e.guides

Earth

LONDON, NEW YORK, MELBOURNE,
MUNICH, and DELHI

Project Editor Nigel Ritchie | **Project Art Editors** Jim Green, Jacqui Swan, Joanna Pocock
Editor Richard Williams | **Senior Designers** Smiljka Surla, Yumiko Tahata
Weblink Editors Clare Lister, Mariza O'Keeffe, | **Illustrators** Mark Longworth, Andrew Kerr, Robin Hunter
Steve Barker, John Bennett | **Cartography** Simon Mumford

Managing Editor Linda Esposito | **Managing Art Editor** Sophia M. Tampakopoulos Turner

Digital Development Manager Fergus Day | **Picture Research** Alison Prior
DTP Coordinator Tony Cutting | **Picture Librarians** Sarah Mills, Rose Horridge,
DTP Designer Pete Quinlan | Karl Stange, Kate Ledwith

Consultant Travis Hudson, Director of Environmental Affairs, | **Production** Erica Rosen
AGI (American Geological Institute) | **Jacket** Neal Cobourne

Category Publisher Sue Grabham | **Art Director** Simon Webb

First American Edition, 2004
Published in the United States by DK Publishing, Inc.
375 Hudson Street, New York, New York 10014

04 05 06 07 08 09 10 9 8 7 6 5 4 3 2 1

Copyright © 2004 Dorling Kindersley Limited
Google™ is a trademark of Google Technology Inc.

Published in Great Britain by Dorling Kindersley Limited.

Library of Congress Cataloging-in-Publication Data

Turner, Matt, 1964-
  E.guides Earth / written by Matt Turner. -- 1st American ed.
      p. cm. -- (DK Google e.guides)
  Includes index.
  ISBN 0-7566-0539 3 (plcj)
  1. Earth--Juvenile Literature. I. Title. II. Series.
  QE501.25.T87 2004
  550--dc22
                                        2004014438

Color reproduction by Media Development and Printing, UK
Printed in China by Toppan Printing Co. (Shenzen) Ltd.

Discover more at
www.dk.com

e.guides

Earth

Written by **Matt Turner**

Google

CONTENTS

HOW TO USE THE WEB SITE	6	DESERTS	54
EARTH IN THE UNIVERSE	8	TROPICAL FORESTS	56
THE SUN AND MOON	10	TEMPERATE FORESTS	58
MAGNETIC EARTH	12	GRASSLANDS	60
EARTH AND LIFE	14	WETLANDS	62
THE AGE OF THE EARTH	16	POLAR REGIONS	64
INSIDE THE EARTH	18	MARINE	66
MOVING EARTH	20	OCEANS	68
EXPLODING EARTH	22	WAVES AND TSUNAMIS	70
RIVERS OF FIRE	24	EL NINO	72
LIVING WITH VOLCANOES	26	EXPLORING OCEAN DEPTHS	74
EARTHQUAKES	28	ATMOSPHERE	76
STUDYING EARTHQUAKES	30	CLIMATE CHANGE	78
SAN ANDREAS FAULT	32	WEATHER	80
MOUNTAIN BUILDING	34	PRECIPITATION	82
LANDSLIDES	36	WEATHER FORECASTING	84
ROCKS	38	TORNADOES	86
MINERALS AND CRYSTALS	40	HURRICANES	88
EROSION	42		
ISLANDS	44	REFERENCE SECTION	
GLACIERS AND ICE SHEETS	46	TIMELINE OF EARTH DISCOVERIES	90
SOIL	48	GLOSSARY	92
RIVERS	50	INDEX	94
CAVES	52	ACKNOWLEDGMENTS	96

How to use the e.guides Web site

e.guides Earth has its own Web site, created by DK and Google™. When you look up a subject in the book, the article gives you key facts and displays a keyword that links you to extra information online. Just follow these easy steps.

http://www.earth.dke-guides.com

1   Enter this Web site address...

Address : @ http://www.earth.dke-guides.com

2   Find the keyword in the book...

caves

3   Enter the keyword...

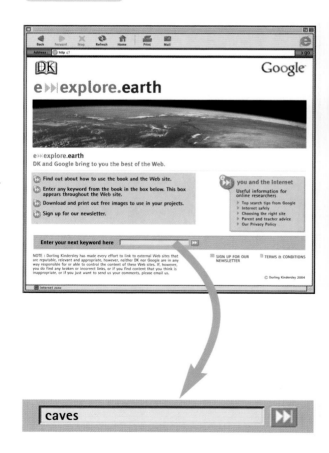

caves

You can use only the keywords from the book to search on our Web site for the specially selected DK/Google links.

Be safe while you are online:

- Always get permission from an adult before connecting to the Internet.

- Never give out personal information about yourself.

- Never arrange to meet someone you have talked to online.

- If a site asks you to log in with your name or email address, ask permission from an adult first.

- Do not reply to emails from strangers—tell an adult.

Parents: Dorling Kindersley actively and regularly reviews and updates the links. However, content may change. Dorling Kindersley is not responsible for any site but its own. We recommend that children are supervised while online, that they do not use chat rooms, and that filtering software is used to block unsuitable material.

Click on your chosen link...

▶▶ Take a virtual tour of a cave

Links include animations, videos, sound buttons, virtual tours, interactive quizzes, databases, timelines, and real-time reports.

Download fantastic pictures...

Pictures | Earth ▶▶

Inside a cave complex

The pictures are free of charge, but can be used for personal noncommercial use only.

Go back to the book for your next subject...

EARTH IN THE UNIVERSE

The Universe is everything that exists—all that we see and touch, all energy, all the stars and planets, and all space. It is enormous, stretching into space for at least 15 billion light-years in every direction. (One light-year is the distance light travels in a year — 5.9 trillion miles or 9.5 trillion km.) The Universe contains countless stars that are clustered in trillions of vast star cities called galaxies. One galaxy is home to our own star—the Sun—and its planets, including Earth.

Universe

BIG BANG ▶
All the galaxies are moving away from one another. This suggests that the Universe was created by an explosion—the Big Bang. In a split-second, the Universe expanded from a speck to a huge fireball of burning gas. Eventually, stars began forming. The Big Bang was 10–20 billion years ago, and most scientists think the Universe will expand forever.

⑨

GALAXIES

ACTIVE GALAXY
All galaxies give off energy. Some, known as active galaxies, give off very large amounts of energy. The energy may take many different forms, including light and radio waves. The energy pours out from an active galaxy's nucleus, which is thought to contain massive objects.

ANDROMEDA
Andromeda is the nearest galaxy to our own galaxy, called the Milky Way. They belong to the same cluster of galaxies, known as the Local Group. Andromeda is about 2 million light years away from Earth. It is a spiral galaxy and contains hundreds of billions of stars.

TRIANGULUM
The Local Group also contains this spiral galaxy, known as Triangulum. It is about a quarter of the size of the Milky Way. Triangulum is believed to be orbiting (moving around) its neighbor Andromeda, which holds the smaller galaxy in the pull of its gravity.

◀ MILKY WAY
The Milky Way is a galaxy of 200 million stars, including our Sun. It is about 100,000 light years wide. It is a spiral galaxy: a thin disc in which dust and stars form arms revolving around a nucleus (center). The Sun lies partway along one arm, which we can see as a pale streak across the night sky. About 70% of all known galaxies are spirals, but some are oval and others are irregular in shape.

AGE OF UNIVERSE (IN BILLIONS OF YEARS)

HORSEHEAD NEBULA ▶

This is a nebula, a cold cloud of swirling dust and gases that are the raw materials of a star. A star is born when a cloud of hydrogen collapses under its own gravity. The cloud spins faster, heats up, and glows as it drags in more gas. Eventually, it gets so hot that it "switches on" and becomes a true star. The light comes from its white-hot core, where nuclear reactions are taking place.

◀ SOLAR SYSTEM

The solar system is made up of the Sun and its 9 planets, as well as countless chunks of rock and ice, such as the asteroid belt that lies in a broad band between Mars and Jupiter. The planets were formed from clouds of rock, dust, and gases orbiting the Sun. The 4 planets closest to the Sun are rocky. The next 4 are larger, with small rocky cores cloaked in gases. Outermost Pluto is a tiny planet of rock and ice.

PLANETS

	PLANET NAME	ORBIT TIME
1	Mercury	88 days
2	Venus	224.7 days
3	Earth	365.3 days
4	Mars	687 days
5	Jupiter	11.9 years
6	Saturn	29.4 years
7	Uranus	84 years
8	Neptune	165 years
9	Pluto	248.6 years

◀ MOON

All the planets except Mercury and Venus are orbited by natural satellites known as moons. The large, gassy planets have many moons: Jupiter, for example, has 61. Earth has just one. The Moon is too small to have an atmosphere like Earth's, so it is lifeless. Its surface is covered with meteorite craters.

EARTH ▼

Earth is the only planet where water can exist at the surface as a liquid, solid, or gas. The oceans and atmosphere provide water and oxygen, vital conditions for life. Also, unlike other planets, Earth is neither too hot nor too cold.

ASTEROID
Asteroids are rocks measuring up to 560 miles (900 km) across. Smaller rocks are called meteors. Comets are chunks of rock, ice, and gas that trail glowing tails when they pass near the Sun.

METEORITE CRATER
Our planet's atmosphere burns up most of the meteors heading for Earth. Every so often, giant rocks get through. They are known as meteorites, and their violent impact leaves a crater.

THE SUN AND MOON

Earth is constantly moving around the Sun, completing an orbit (circuit) every year. At the same time, it rotates on its own axis, a little like a spinning top. Together, planet Earth's motions control how its surface is exposed to the Sun's heat and light. They govern the daily rhythm of day and night, the length of each year, and the seasons. The motions are so regular that we set our clocks and live our lives by them. Meanwhile, Earth has its own orbiting body, the Moon, which completes a circuit every month. The pull of its gravity is strong enough to create Earth's ocean tides.

Southern autumnal and northern vernal (spring) equinox

Earth's axis

North Pole

Northern summer, southern winter (North Pole tilts toward Sun)

HOLE IN THE OZONE LAYER
Ozone, a form of oxygen found in Earth's atmosphere, protects our health by absorbing harmful radiation. In the 1970s, scientists reported that industrial chemicals known as CFCs were thinning the ozone. In 1985, a hole in the ozone layer was detected over Antarctica. Use of CFCs is now banned.

DAY AND NIGHT ▶
Every 24 hours, Earth makes one rotation around an imaginary line called its axis—a straight line through the poles. This brings daylight to the regions facing the Sun and night to those facing away. Earth rotates in an easterly direction, which means that the Sun always rises over the eastern horizon. Earth's axis is not at right angles to its orbit around the Sun; it is tilted over at an angle of 23.5 degrees from the vertical.

Direction of Earth's spin

RADIATION FROM THE SUN

5% scattered back into space by atmosphere

20% reflected back by clouds

15% absorbed by clouds and atmosphere

5% reflected by surface

5% absorbed by water, dust, and gases in the air

50% absorbed by surface

◀ EARTH'S SEASONS
Earth's axis is tilted toward the Sun, creating different levels of sunlight—which we experience as seasons. When sunlight falls directly on the exposed hemisphere (northern or southern) the day is longer, creating summer conditions. When that pole faces away, sunlight is weaker and the days are shorter, creating winter conditions. At any point in the year, each hemisphere is experiencing opposing seasons.

NORWAY'S MIDNIGHT SUN
The summer Sun is seen at midnight in northern Norway. The far north gets more hours of sunlight than usual during the 6 months in each year when the North Pole is tilted toward the Sun. In high summer, lands in the Arctic Circle enjoy sunlight for 24 hours a day. In midwinter, the Sun does not appear at all.

◀ SOLAR RADIATION
Earth absorbs heat and light from the Sun. Other forms of solar energy reach us too. They include short-wave, high-energy radiation, like gamma rays, x-rays, and ultraviolet (UV) light. This radiation is harmful. For example, UV can give us skin cancers and damage our eyes. The layers of Earth's atmosphere protect us from damage. Earth's upper atmosphere reflects gamma rays and x-rays back into space. Below this, the ozone layer absorbs most of the UV light.

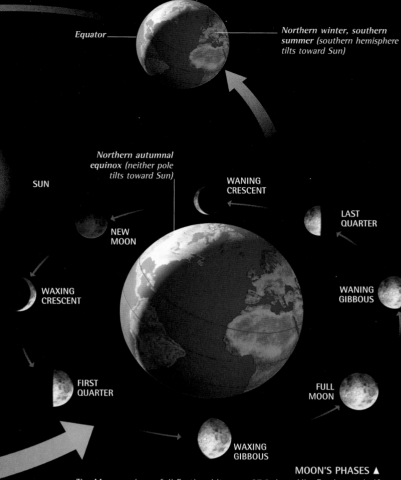

Equator

Northern winter, southern **summer** (southern hemisphere tilts toward Sun)

SUN

Northern autumnal **equinox** (neither pole tilts toward Sun)

WANING CRESCENT

NEW MOON

LAST QUARTER

WAXING CRESCENT

WANING GIBBOUS

FIRST QUARTER

FULL MOON

WAXING GIBBOUS

MOON'S PHASES ▲

The Moon makes a full Earth orbit every 27.3 days. Like Earth, one half of the Moon is always in sunlight. But because the Moon is constantly changing its position relative to the Sun and Earth, every night we see a different proportion of sunlight on the Moon's surface. In the course of a month, the Moon waxes (grows) from a thin crescent to a full moon and then wanes (shrinks) again until the "new moon" position, when the sunlit part is facing away from us and none of it is visible.

TEMPERATE SEASONS

SPRING
Temperate lands lying between the tropics (the regions on either side of the equator) and the poles have 4 distinct seasons. In the northern hemisphere, March 21 or 22 is the vernal (spring) equinox: a date when the Sun shines directly on the equator. Now days become longer and warmer, stimulating plant growth.

SUMMER
Summer is the warmest season. In the northern hemisphere, summer occurs between June and September, and in the southern hemisphere, between December and February. On June 21 or 22 , the North Pole is at its maximum tilt toward the Sun. In the northern hemisphere, this is the longest day of the year.

FALL
In the fall, the days grow cooler and longer. The opposite of the vernal equinox is the autumnal equinox, which falls in the northern hemisphere on September 22 or 23. The shortening hours of daylight lead to a slowdown in plant growth, and many trees shed their leaves in preparation for winter.

WINTER
Winter is the coldest season. On December 21 or 22 (known in the northern hemisphere as the winter solstice), the North Pole is at its maximum tilt away from the Sun. The cold and darkness make some animals hibernate. Others migrate to the southern hemisphere, which is experiencing the warmth of a summer solstice.

Sun and Moon

SUN

SUN

MOON

EARTH

MOON

EARTH

NEAP TIDE (LOWEST)

SPRING TIDE (HIGHEST)

◄ EARTH'S OCEAN TIDES

Every day, Earth's coastlines are washed by the tide—a regular rise and fall in the sea level. As the Moon orbits Earth, the oceans facing it are pulled by lunar gravity, creating a bulge. This brings high tide: a rise in water levels. There is also a matching bulge on the side of Earth facing away from the Moon, caused by the centrifugal force of Earth's rotation. Earth's rotation creates 2 high and 2 low tides every 24 hours. When the Moon and the Sun are in line (twice a month), the combined pull of their gravity creates extra high tides, known as spring tides. Neap tides occur when the gravitational pull of the Moon is weakest.

MAGNETIC EARTH

Magnetism is an invisible force that attracts or repels certain materials, such as iron. The outer part of Earth's hot core is made up mostly of liquid iron. Heat makes the iron swirl around in such a way that it becomes magnetic, turning Earth into a giant magnet. Like any other magnet, Earth has magnetic north and south poles. These lie close to the geographic North and South poles. Earth's magnetism helps us find our way by using a compass, and it also helps guide some animals when they migrate over long distances.

magnetic Earth

AURORA ON JUPITER

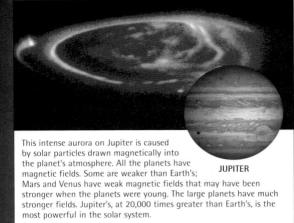

JUPITER

This intense aurora on Jupiter is caused by solar particles drawn magnetically into the planet's atmosphere. All the planets have magnetic fields. Some are weaker than Earth's; Mars and Venus have weak magnetic fields that may have been stronger when the planets were young. The large planets have much stronger fields. Jupiter's, at 20,000 times greater than Earth's, is the most powerful in the solar system.

Solar wind: charged particles from the Sun

EARTH'S MAGNETOSPHERE ▶
Earth's magnetic field, known as the magnetosphere (whose boundary is shown in purple), reaches far into space. It protects us from the solar wind: a stream of harmful rays that pours from the Sun. When the rays hit the magnetosphere, they are slowed down and pushed aside, though some are drawn toward the poles. Pressure from the solar wind changes the shape of the magnetosphere, giving it a blunt head and a long tail that streams off into space.

Bow shock helps force the solar wind to go around the magnetosphere

◀ AURORA AUSTRALIS
Charged particles from the Sun also affect southern skies, where the lights are known as the aurora australis. At both poles, the light effect often hangs like a vast curtain, but also appears in patches and bands. Auroras are most spectacular when the Sun is particularly active. At these times, massive, violent outbursts of solar energy flood Earth's atmosphere and can cause electrical storms as well.

▲ AURORA BOREALIS
This glow in the northern night sky is the aurora borealis, or northern lights. It is caused by electrically charged particles that pour from the Sun at speeds of about 250 miles/sec (400 km/sec). Particles that get close to the polar regions are drawn into the atmosphere by Earth's magnetic field. The disturbed magnetic field flings the particles trapped in it toward Earth, making the upper air glow around the poles.

MODERN
COMPASS

◄ MAGNETIC NORTH
A compass is simply a
device with a magnetized
needle that points to
magnetic north, swinging
freely on a pivot. The
needle lines up with
Earth's magnetic field so
that its tips always point to
Earth's magnetic poles. The
Chinese developed the compass
in the 11th century. Their compass
pointed to Earth's magnetic south pole.
Europeans and Arabs preferred their compass
to point to Earth's magnetic north pole.

MAGNETITE WITH
IRON FILINGS

▲ MAGNETIC ROCK
Magnetite, a common
source of iron, is a
naturally magnetic mineral. It is
magnetized by Earth as it lies in the
ground. Magnetite is a permanent
magnet: it does not lose its magnetism.
This is unlike temporary magnets, such
as pieces of pure iron, which slowly
lose their magnetism after being
removed from a forcefield.

COMPASS NAVIGATION
The Ancient Chinese knew
about magnetite's unusual
qualities in the 4th century BC,
but did not develop the
compass until the 11th
century, when they discovered
they could use magnetite to
magnetize an iron or steel
needle. Europeans and Arabs
discovered this independently
more than 100 years later.

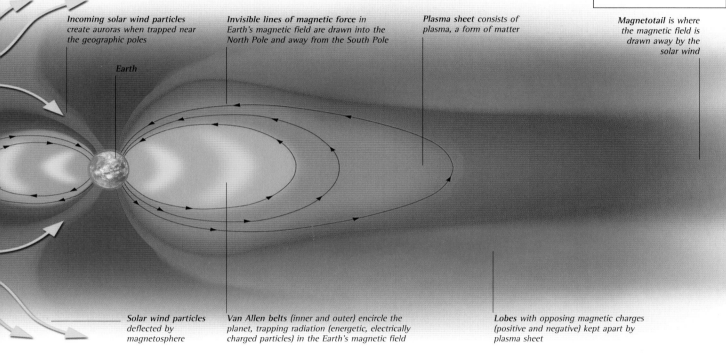

Incoming solar wind particles
create auroras when trapped near
the geographic poles

Invisible lines of magnetic force in
Earth's magnetic field are drawn into the
North Pole and away from the South Pole

Plasma sheet consists of
plasma, a form of matter

Magnetotail is where
the magnetic field is
drawn away by the
solar wind

Earth

Solar wind particles
deflected by
magnetosphere

Van Allen belts (inner and outer) encircle the
planet, trapping radiation (energetic, electrically
charged particles) in the Earth's magnetic field

Lobes with opposing magnetic charges
(positive and negative) kept apart by
plasma sheet

LOGGERHEAD TURTLE MIGRATION ROUTE

Loggerhead turtles probably
use magnetism to find their
way in the Atlantic Ocean.
After hatching on Florida
beaches, baby turtles scuttle
toward the waves. Many then
spend several years cruising
warm currents. A magnetic
sense helps them avoid the
prevailing northeastern
currents heading for Britain,
and they continue southward
down the coast of Africa
before returning as adults to
Florida to breed.

NORTH
AMERICA

ATLANTIC
OCEAN

FLORIDA

WESTERN
AFRICA

PACIFIC
OCEAN

SOUTH
AMERICA

KEY TO MAP

●   Starting point for loggerhead turtle migration

→   Ocean currents

⇢   Migration route

▲ BEACHED WHALE
Whales regularly become stranded on beaches, either singly or
in pods (groups). It has been suggested that they use Earth's
magnetic field to navigate while on migration, and this system
sometimes lets them down. Though there is no firm proof,
research in the 1980s suggested that fin whales may lose their
way in areas of weak magnetism. Whales that lose their way may
blunder onto a surprise obstacle, such as a low sandbank.

EARTH AND LIFE

Life depends on water in all its forms. Earth is the only planet with water, and the only one known to support life. Earth's temperature is just right for water to be present in the atmosphere, oceans, soil, and icecaps. Covering the planet is a thin layer of life, known as the biosphere. This total life system includes all plants and animals, as well as the nonliving materials that form part of the cycle of life.

BLUE PLANET ▶
From space, Earth is a shimmering blue planet covered in water, and swirling with clouds – evidence of our precious atmosphere. The gases that make up the atmosphere, mostly nitrogen and oxygen, are held in place by gravity. They form a very thin layer, like an envelope around the surface.

biosphere

SUN ▶
Water alone is not enough to support life, energy from the Sun is also needed. Plants use sunlight to fuel photosynthesis, the process by which they turn carbon dioxide (CO_2) and water into nutrients. Earth's atmosphere blocks harmful solar energy from reaching the planet, while absorbing sufficient heat and light to nurture life.

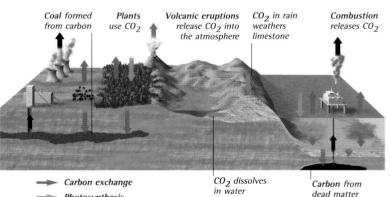

Coal formed from carbon

Plants use CO_2

Volcanic eruptions release CO_2 into the atmosphere

CO_2 in rain weathers limestone

Combustion releases CO_2

CO_2 dissolves in water

Carbon from dead matter forms oil and gas

◀ CARBON CYCLE
Next to water, organic compounds (compounds containing the element carbon) are the most important ingredient of life-forms. Earth's carbon supply is stored in rocks, soil, water, and the atmosphere, as well as in plant and animal tissue. It is readily converted from one form to another, and is recycled constantly through all parts of the biosphere.

➡ Carbon exchange
➡ Photosynthesis
➡ Weathering and erosion
➡ Human carbon transformation

◀ OCEANS
The salty oceans contain about 96.5% of Earth's water. Of the 3.5% that is fresh (not salty), 1.7% is stored in polar ice, and a similar amount lies in or on the land, such as in rivers and lakes. A tiny amount drifts in the atmosphere. We cannot do without water, since it makes up about 60% by weight of our bodies and plays a role in every biological function.

Plants lose water through transpiration (evaporating from their leaves)

Clouds carry water inland to fall as rain and snow

◀ WATER CYCLE
Water is constantly on the move as a result of solar energy. It evaporates from the oceans, and moves through the atmosphere toward land, where it falls as rain or snow. Some then runs off the surface to form rivers and lakes, which return water to the ocean or the atmosphere. A large amount of rainfall soaks through gaps in the soil to be stored in a vast underground water system.

Rivers and streams return water to seas and oceans

BIOMES

The biosphere is not spread evenly around the planet. Levels of sunlight, temperature, and rainfall differ from one place to another. So, too, do air and ocean currents and land altitudes. The varied conditions create a mosaic of climates, each with its own community of life-forms. Scientists class the communities in groups called biomes, some of which are shown below.

- ☐ Polar
- ☐ Grassland
- ☐ Temperate forest
- ☐ Tropical forest
- ☐ Desert
- ☐ Wetland
- ☐ Coral reef

FORESTS ▶

Trees have adapted to survive many climates, from the warm, wet tropics to the cold North. Today, forests cover a quarter of the planet's land area. The richest of all biomes, forests are home to at least 50% of the world's species. They produce nearly half the world's total organic matter and contain about half its total carbon store. Forests prevent soil from being washed away by rain. They also act as Earth's lungs by producing oxygen from carbon dioxide, restoring oxygen levels in the atmosphere.

DESERTS ▶

Deserts include the world's driest lands. They may be hot or cold—even icy—but all are very dry. Nevertheless, life adapts to tough conditions. Plants may grow long roots to reach water deep underground, or lie inactive for years until sudden, brief showers allow them to flower and seed. Desert animals tend to be active at night in order to escape the Sun. Desert ecosystems are very fragile, and overgrazing by livestock may be expanding deserts in sub-Saharan Africa and Central Asia.

GRASSLANDS ▶

Grasslands receive too little rainfall for forest cover, but enough for grasses and shrubs. The plants are adapted to survive poor-quality soil, frequent droughts, and fires. Grasslands include dry grasslands, scrublands, and shrublands. The savannas of sub-Saharan Africa, where grassy plains have a light scattering of trees, are home to rich communities of grazing animals and meat-eaters. Mediterranean-type shrubland grows in climates with cool, wet winters and hot, dry summers.

POLAR REGIONS ▶

The polar regions are the coldest regions on Earth. Antarctica, the southern continent, is cut off from the other landmasses by the stormy Southern Ocean. It is an almost lifeless desert, covered in ice and snow. The Arctic Ocean has a milder climate, especially during the summer, when the tundra teems with life. At both poles, the ocean waters have a high oxygen content, supporting a wide community of animals.

THE AGE OF THE EARTH

Our planet is more than 4.5 billion years old. How do we know this? Geologists study Earth's rocks in order to learn about events that happened in the distant past. They use important changes as markers to divide the planet's long history into several time periods. Placed in a row, the markers make up the geologic timescale. Geologists use this scale to compare their discoveries and understand the history of Earth.

◀ ARGON DATING
Modern radiometric dating helps to determine the absolute age of rocks. Some elements of rocks are radioactive: they break apart and turn into other elements. For instance, potassium-40 breaks down into argon-40. Geologists know how fast it breaks down, so they can date a rock by measuring how much argon-40 it contains.

EARLY LIFE
About 543 million years ago, life on Earth suddenly flourished, as shown by the amazing range of fossils found from that time onward. For the first time, animals had hard body parts, which not only helped them survive but also fossilized well. This picture shows a trilobite: sea-bed scavengers that teemed in the Cambrian oceans.

FOSSIL ALGAE
The planet's oldest known life-forms are tiny, one-celled organisms such as bacteria and algae. You would need a microscope to study these two-billion-year-old fossil algae found in Precambrian rocks from North America.

e ▸▸ Earth's timeline

▲ VOLCANIC BEGINNINGS
At first, the Earth's surface was so hot that it was liquid. As it cooled, the rock hardened. Volcanoes spewed out molten rock and gases: carbon dioxide, nitrogen, and water vapour. Rainfall from the vapour created the oceans. Carbon dioxide dissolved into the oceans, where the first life-forms turned the gas into oxygen.

▲ STROMATOLITES
Stromatolites are mats formed from the dead bodies of algae. The algae live in colonies in shallow water and use sunlight to make energy. Stromatolites are some of the world's oldest fossils, found in rocks up to 3.5 billion years old. Living stromatolites can still be found today in Australia and North America.

EON	PRECAMBRIAN – FIRST LANDMASSES						
ERA		PALAEOZOIC – AGE OF ANCIENT LIFE					
PERIOD		CAMBRIAN	ORDOVICIAN	SILURIAN	DEVONIAN	CARBONIFEROUS	PERMIAN
EPOCH						MISSISSIPPIAN / PENNSYLVANIAN	
	4,560 million years ago (mya)	544 mya	495 mya	443 mya	417 mya	354 mya / 323 mya	290 mya

◀ METEORITE CRATER

Mass extinctions occur in Earth's history when many life-forms die out at once. The age of dinosaurs may have been ended by a huge meteorite that struck the Yucatan peninsula in Mexico, 65 million years ago. Dust clouds rising from the impact would have blotted out the Sun's light for years, killing plants and dinosaurs.

◀ WOOLLY MAMMOTH

This mammoth calf was dug up in Siberia in 1977. It is not a fossil, but the whole animal. Ice in the frozen soil kept it from rotting when it died. Mammoths looked like elephants, but with more hair and smaller ears. They roamed the northern grasslands until a cooling climate and hunting by humans killed them off about 11,000 years ago.

FOSSIL RECORD

Fossils are an important tool for understanding Earth's history. They enable us to study extinct animals that lived a long time ago. Because rock layers from different periods contain different fossils, scientists can use fossils to discover how Earth has changed. This geologist is excavating a dinosaur fossil in the southwest United States.

HOMO SAPIENS SKULL

Human-like skulls and footprints found in Africa date back 4.5 million years. They suggest our ancestors were short, ape-like, and walked on hind legs. Modern humans – *Homo sapiens* – appeared just 130,000 years ago. If Earth's history to date were squeezed into one day, we arrived at two seconds to midnight!

▲ JURASSIC FERNS

Ferns are ancient plants that date back more than 300 million years. This rainforest in Washington State has many ferns like those of the Jurassic period, when dinosaurs lumbered through ferny undergrowth to feed on cone-bearing and palm-like trees. There were, however, no flowering plants in the Jurassic period.

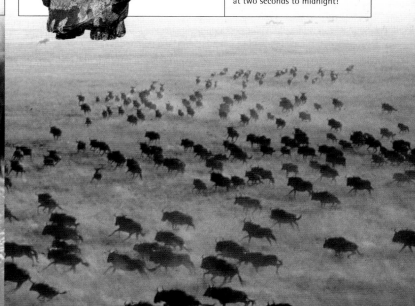

▲ GRAZING MAMMALS

Mammals took over when the dinosaurs died out. Their age, the Cenozoic era, began 65 million years ago and continues today. They inherited a cooler world with flowering plants and grasses. New kinds of mammals evolved to live on open plains. They had chopping and grinding teeth and legs designed for running.

PHANEROZOIC — AGE OF ABUNDANT EVIDENT LIFE

MESOZOIC — AGE OF DOMINANT REPTILES				CENOZOIC — AGE OF DOMINANT MAMMALS							
TRIASSIC	JURASSIC	CRETACEOUS		TERTIARY					QUATERNARY		
		LOWER	UPPER	PALAEOCENE	EOCENE	OLIGOCENE	MIOCENE	PLIOCENE	PLEISTOCENE	HOLOCENE	
251 mya	206 mya	142 mya	99 mya	65 mya	55 mya	34 mya	24 mya	5.3 mya	1.8 mya	0.01 mya	Today

INSIDE THE EARTH

Earth is made up of different layers, which formed when the planet was young and extremely hot. The main layers are the core at the center, then the mantle, and finally the crust on which we live. Earth is still very hot today. The heat creates flow in the inner molten rock layers, causing plates—pieces of the brittle crust—to slide around over them. Evidence of this active, changing planet can be seen at the surface: the movement of the plates creates volcanoes and earthquakes. In fact, it was through studying earthquake tremors that scientists discovered the existence of Earth's layers.

inside Earth

Upper mantle: partly molten rock, 416 miles (670 km) thick; temp. 1,800°F (1,000°C)

Lower mantle: solid rock, 1,385 miles (2,230 km) thick; temp. 6,300°F (3,500°C)

Outer core: liquid metals, c. 1,400 miles (2,250 km) thick; temp. 7,200°F (4,000°C)

Inner core: solid metals, c. 1515 miles (2,440 km) across; temp. 12,600°F (7,000°C)

Oceanic crust: solid basalt, 5 miles (8 km) thick; temp. up to 1,800°F (1,000°C)

Continental crust: solid rock (various), up to 45 miles (70 km) thick; temp. up to 1,800°F (1,000°C)

▲ EARTH'S LAYERS

Earth was originally a fusion of hot, molten gas and dust. Lighter elements floated to the surface and cooled to form the crust. Heavier elements, such as iron and nickel, sank to the core. Mantle rocks have a basaltlike composition. The upper mantle is near melting point and flows slowly. Greater pressure deeper down makes the lower mantle more solid. Likewise, metals are molten in the outer core, but are made solid in the inner core as a result of immense pressure.

▼ CRUSTAL LANDSCAPE FEATURES

The lithosphere is Earth's rigid shell, combining the crust with the uppermost mantle layer. It is broken into many separate plates. Heat from deep inside Earth creates currents in the mantle below, which cause the plates to slide around in different directions. In some places they collide head-on, and in others they grind alongside one another or drift apart.

FEATURES OF THE EARTH'S CRUST

1. **Continental crust:** made up of various rock types, and thicker than oceanic crust
2. **Basin:** wide depressions formed in front of elevated areas and filled with sediment
3. **Colliding continental plates:** the crust is stacked up along faults
4. **Uplifted mountain range:** continental collision piles up rock to form high mountain range
5. **Oceanic crust:** several times thinner than continental crust, but made of heavier basalt
6. **Upper mantle:** partly molten; solid uppermost part combines with crust to form lithosphere
7. **Lower mantle:** solid, dense rock such as peridotite below the upper mantle
8. **Spreading oceanic plates:** as they move apart, lava rises to form a midoceanic ridge
9. **Mantle hot spot:** volcanoes form islands where magma rises from the mantle
10. **Trench:** created at subduction zone as oceanic plate sinks below lighter continental plate
11. **Subduction zone:** formed where plates converge and one sinks below the other
12. **Stratovolcano:** formed above subduction zone from magma generated in mantle below
13. **Rift valley:** crust pulls apart, and the land between drops, creating a valley

MOLTEN IRON (CORE)
No samples of Earth's core have been studied, but it is thought to be made up mostly of iron, along with a little nickel. Both metals are very dense and heavy, and they sank beneath other materials early in Earth's history: the core was the first of the planet's layers to form. Today, iron makes up about 35% of Earth's total mass. Heat and planetary rotation make molten iron swirl around the outer core. This motion generates the planet's magnetic field.

PERIDOTITE (MANTLE)
Peridotite is a dark, heavy rock made mainly from olivine and pyroxene. Samples of the rock have been ejected from deep below ground during volcanic eruptions. They show that the mantle is made up of olivine and other minerals containing magnesium, iron, and silica. Scientists have squeezed olivine in the laboratory and found that its crystals pack more solidly under pressure, as seen in this microscopic close-up of a thin slice of peridotite.

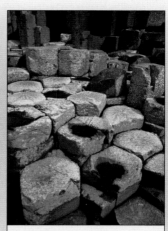

BASALT (CRUST)
Basalt is a fine-grained, heavy volcanic rock. It is formed from magma, which flows up from the mantle into gaps between diverging crustal plates. It is the most common rock on Earth's surface. Basalt can erupt on continents (as seen above in these basalt columnar formations) but it also forms the oceanic crust. No part of the basalt ocean floor is older than 200 million years, because the rock is constantly being consumed in subduction zones.

MOVING EARTH

The Earth is moving beneath our feet. Its hard shell, the lithosphere, is made up of the crust and the hard, uppermost part of the upper mantle. It is broken into 17 plates that drift on the asthenosphere, the semimolten part of the upper mantle. The word used to describe the movement of Earth's plates is tectonics. The plates beneath the oceans are quite thin but are made of heavy material, while continental plates are made from lighter, thicker material. Some plates are sliding past one another, some are coming together, and others are moving apart. The boundaries where plates meet are where many of Earth's most interesting features occur, in the form of mountain ranges, volcanoes, ocean trenches, and earthquakes.

tectonics

▼ CONVERGING PLATES: HIMALAYAS
The Himalaya mountains in central Asia were created when two continental plates converged, or collided. About 50 million years ago the plate carrying India drifted northeastward into the Eurasian mainland. If it had been a heavy oceanic plate, it would have sunk beneath the Eurasian Plate. Since both plates were continental, they were too thick and light for one to sink beneath the other. The northern edge of the Indian Plate crumpled, pushing up the Himalayas.

Mountains formed by two continental plates colliding

Eurasian Plate

Indian Plate

PLATE BOUNDARIES

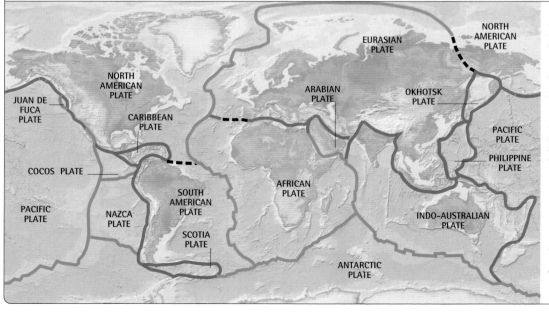

NORTH AMERICAN PLATE

EURASIAN PLATE

NORTH AMERICAN PLATE

JUAN DE FUCA PLATE

ARABIAN PLATE

OKHOTSK PLATE

CARIBBEAN PLATE

PACIFIC PLATE

PHILIPPINE PLATE

COCOS PLATE

PACIFIC PLATE

NAZCA PLATE

SOUTH AMERICAN PLATE

AFRICAN PLATE

INDO-AUSTRALIAN PLATE

SCOTIA PLATE

ANTARCTIC PLATE

Plate boundaries fall into three groups: convergent (moving together), divergent (moving apart), and transform (sliding past one another). The boundaries are where most of Earth's major earthquakes take place. Really big earthquakes are especially common along convergent and transform boundaries. Volcanoes are also common at the convergent boundaries around the Pacific coastline. Most divergent boundaries lie along midocean ridges, where the gap they leave is plugged by basalt magma (molten rock) rising from the mantle below and cooling to form new solid crust on the ocean floor.

KEY TO MAP

——— *convergent boundary*

——— *divergent boundary*

——— *transform fault*

- - - - - *uncertain boundary*

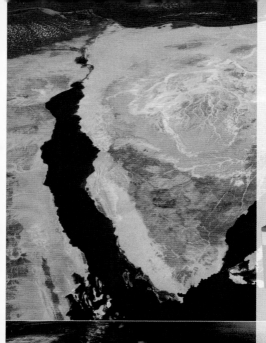

◄ DIVERGENT BOUNDARY
The Red Sea has divided East Africa and Arabia since the African and Arabian Plates began diverging some 50 million years ago. As the plates parted, great slabs of land slipped down into the gap in a series of faults. Later, the gap (or rift) filled with seawater. The Red Sea rift connects to the midocean ridge of the Indian Ocean.

Plates pull apart

Magma rises from mantle

◄ CONVERGENT BOUNDARY
The Andes in South America form a volcanic mountain range created by subduction—an oceanic plate sinking under a continental plate at a convergent boundary. As the Nazca Plate went under the South American Plate, it sank into the mantle, causing parts of the overlying mantle to melt and form magma. The magma then rose through the crust to form volcanoes.

Continental plate

Mountain range

Oceanic plate pushed under

◄ TRANSFORM FAULT
The San Andreas Fault, on the US Pacific coast, marks a transform boundary. The Pacific and North American Plates are sliding past one another, but rock friction causes them to stick for long periods. Tension gradually builds up, and the sudden movement as they slip past one another creates a violent shock—an earthquake. A major earthquake on this fault, in 1906, caused fires that engulfed central San Francisco.

Earthquakes caused when two plates slip

MOVING CONTINENTS
The German geophysicist Alfred Wegener (1880–1930) was one of the first to suggest that continents moved. The opposing coastlines of the South Atlantic Ocean looked similar to him. He reasoned that the edges of the major landmasses could be put back together, like a jigsaw puzzle. His idea was not widely accepted until the 1960s.

PANGAEA
The plates of the lithosphere have been in motion since they first formed 3.5 billion years ago. These movements have brought continents together, split them apart, and reshaped oceans. Wegener's assembled jigsaw, named Pangaea, shows how the landmasses would have looked 200 million years ago, in the time of the early dinosaurs.

DRIFTING CONTINENTS
One hundred million years later, Pangaea lay in pieces. Divergent plates had begun to open up the Atlantic Ocean. South America was drifting west. Antarctica was heading for the South Pole. Off the eastern coast of Africa, India was creeping northeast toward Asia.

THE EARTH TODAY
Today's map shows India in place after it collided with the Eurasian mainland. Greenland has separated from North America, which now has a land bridge with South America. Australia has drifted into the Pacific. In 100 million years the map will look quite different.

PROOF OF SHIFTING PLATES ►
Rocks have provided evidence for the theory of Earth's moving plates. Fossils of *Glossopteris*, an ancient plant, had been found in India, Australia, Africa, and South America. These lands, now far apart, must have been joined 250 million years ago, in *Glossopteris's* day. Likewise, fossils of *Mesosaurus*, a freshwater reptile that lived 280 million years ago, have been found only on the Atlantic coasts of Africa and South America.

MESOSAURUS FOSSIL

Seed fern

GLOSSOPTERIS FOSSIL

EXPLODING EARTH

About four-fifths of Earth's total surface is volcanic rock. It rose through the crust as magma (molten rock) from the upper mantle, before emerging in the form of lava, which then cooled and hardened. Volcanoes are visible proof of an active, changing planet. They are most common at tectonic plate boundaries. Where two oceanic plates move apart, relatively gentle eruptions produce long volcanic ridges on the seafloor. But where an oceanic plate sinks beneath another plate, chains of stratovolcanoes form. Stratovolcanoes have highly explosive eruptions capable of causing widespread devastation.

volcanoes

STRATOVOLCANO ▶
Magma rises through cracks and builds up in chambers. Eventually, pressure from below forces it up to the surface to erupt. Very runny lava, with a low gas and silica content, erupts in gushing rivers. Very sticky lava, with a high gas and silica content, erupts explosively. It blasts out pyroclastic materials (clouds of ash made up of powdered rock and fragments of volcanic glass) and blobs of lava. Explosive volcanoes that eject both pyroclastic materials and lava are called stratovolcanoes.

8

7

6

2

5

2

3

GLOBAL VOLCANIC ACTIVITY (FAMOUS VOLCANOES)

MOUNT ST HELENS   MOUNT VESUVIUS ▲

▲ MAUNA LOA   MOUNT PINATUBO ▲

TAMBORA

NAME	MAJOR ERUPTION	PLACE
Mauna Loa	Continuous	Hawaii
Mount Pinatubo	1991	Luzon, Philippines
Mount St Helens	1980	Washington State
Tambora	1815	Sundas, Indonesia
Mount Vesuvius	AD 79	Pompeii, Italy

1

▲ MOUNT ST. HELENS, WASHINGTON STATE

Mount St. Helens, erupted with explosive force in 1980. This ancient stratovolcano had started showing signs of activity in March, in step with a series of earthquakes in the region. On May 18, a quake triggered a massive landslide and Mount St. Helens erupted. Almost 0.24 cubic miles (1 km³) of rock was blown into the air, and the peak was left shorter by 1,350 ft (400 m).

Shield volcano: runny lava produces gently sloping sides

▲ MAUNA LOA, HAWAII

Mauna Loa on Hawaii Island is the world's largest volcano, rising more than 11 miles (17 km) from its base. The volcanoes that make up the Hawaiian Island chain (most of which are underwater) stretch 1,500 miles (2,400 km) across the Pacific Ocean, and were formed as the Pacific Plate moved over a fixed "hot spot." It is a shield volcano, a gently sloping mound built up by repeated eruptions of runny lava. Unlike stratovolcanoes, shield volcanoes seldom erupt explosively.

Fissure eruption: lava flows from opening due to weak crust

▲ PITON DE LA FOURNAISE, REUNION

The Piton de la Fournaise on Réunion Island is a basaltic volcano, formed by a hot spot, and one of the most active volcanoes on Earth, erupting roughly once every two years. Réunion Island forms the tip of a huge volcano rising from the ocean floor, which was created by a hot spot in the Indian Ocean off the east coast of Madagascar. During eruptions, fissure vents often open up on the flanks of Piton de la Fournaise, sending out fluid red-hot lava flows; the crusted black lava creeps along at a much slower rate.

STRATOVOLCANO

1. **Asthenosphere:** lower layer of upper mantle containing partially molten rock
2. **Lithosphere:** Earth's solid outer layer (crust combined with uppermost layer of the upper mantle)
3. **Magma chamber:** a reservoir in the crust filled by rising magma from below
4. **Pluton:** a buried mass of igneous rock that forms when magma in an old chamber cools and hardens
5. **Pipe:** the vertical channel through the crust by which magma reaches the surface
6. **Composite layers:** deposits of lava and pyroclastic material from earlier eruptions
7. **Vent:** the opening at the surface from which volcanic materials are ejected; some volcanoes have several
8. **Pyroclastic flow:** a hot—and deadly—cloud of ash and gases that flows very rapidly down the sides
9. **Lava:** river of molten rock (magma is known as lava when it reaches the surface)
10. **Caldera:** a crater that forms when the walls of the vent collapse, usually after a violent eruption

Some volcanic eruptions are violent explosions of lava, gas, and ash. At the other extreme, the volcanoes on Hawaii pour out huge fountains and rivers of lava but cause little damage. What puts the bang in a volcano? The answer lies in the lava. The explosive form, known as rhyolitic or andesitic lava, is typically hot and sticky. It may contain many volatiles (dissolved gases) and silica. The lava on, for instance, Hawaii is of the basaltic form: very hot and runny, and relatively low in silica and volatiles.

volcanoes

STROMBOLIAN ERUPTION ON MOUNT ETNA, SICILY ▲
A Strombolian explosion is when a volcano repeatedly sends jets of fluid lava into the air, after the active volcano on Stromboli, an island off Sicily. The gases released from volcanoes, such as steam and carbon dioxide, are called volatiles. While magma remains deep below ground, pressure keeps the volatiles dissolved. As the magma rises, the pressure drops and the volatiles escape—similar to when you open a carbonated drink. The bubbling volatiles blow the magma into fragments as it is ejected from the volcano.

▼ LAVA LAKE IN KILAUEA CRATER, HAWAII
Kilauea on Hawaii is one of the most active and studied volcanoes in the world. It is a typical shield volcano, whose shallow cone shape is built up from many layers of basaltic lava produced by frequent but gentle eruptions, often from several vents (openings) in the slopes and crater. Fluid lava is usually associated with ocean floor and hot spot activity, such as that found under Hawaii. Basaltic lava often spreads over a wide area before solidifying.

Caldera (sunken crater) filled with basaltic lava

Basaltic lava has low silica content but extremely high temperatures

Vulcanologist   *Roof formed by crust of cooled lava*   *River of lava flowing through tube*

▲ ROOFED LAVA TUBE, HAWAII
Lava tubes form from rivers of very hot and runny lava, usually the basaltic type. When lava flows down a narrow gulley, the skin on its surface may harden into a roof. Under the roof, a tube of hot lava continues to flow. Tube roofs frequently collapse in places, as this example on Hawaii has done. When lava tubes drain dry, they become volcanic caves that can be explored.

BASALT COLUMNS IN NAMIBIA ▶
Basalt lava sometimes cools naturally into many-sided columns. This picture shows a volcanic rock formation from Twyfelfontein, Namibia, known as the "Organ Pipes," after their perpendicular shape and arrangement. These pillars, made from dolerite (a type of basalt), formed around 120 million year ago. Distinctive basalt columns can also be found on the northern coast of Ireland (the "Giant's Causeway") and in Iceland.

YPES OF BASALT LAVA

PILLOW LAVA
When an underwater volcano erupts, it often creates pillow lava on the sea-bed. As lava comes into contact with the cold water it quickly forms a thick skin, which allows the lava inside each "pillow"' to cool relatively slowly. If you find pillow lava on dry land it is a sure sign that the area once lay underwater.

PAHOEHOE LAVA
Pahoehoe (pronounced "pah-hoy-hoy") is the Hawaiian word for "ropey." It is common in Hawaiian eruptions. This very fluid lava erupts in thin sheets that flow rapidly over large areas. It forms a smooth, stretchy skin that is drawn into ropelike folds and globules as the molten lava flows beneath it.

AA LAVA
Aa (pronounced "ah-ah") is another common form of Hawaiian lava. Cooler than pahoehoe, it is also sticky and slower-flowing. A thick skin forms, which crumbles as it oozes along. The slivers and chunks have dangerously jagged edges, which make it impossible to walk on in bare feet. This may explain how the lava got its name!

▲ GEOTHERMAL ENERGY, ICELAND
Natural hot springs are common in highly volcanic regions, where underground lakes of magma lie close to Earth's surface. As water seeps deep into the ground, it is heated by the magma and by the high pressure at great depths. It rises again as steam, shooting from the ground in scalding fountains called geysers or bubbling into mineral-rich lakes. This lake in Iceland doubles as a source of geothermal ("Earth-heated") energy and as a relaxing hotpool.

LIVING WITH VOLCANOES

Today, roughly half a billion people live near a volcano. Many of them risk being killed by an eruption or its after-effects. Why do they stay? One reason is that volcanic ash makes land fertile and good for farming. In any case, volcanoes may be dormant (inactive) for years between eruptions. Even so, scientists watch volcanoes carefully for warning signs of danger. Volcanoes can be the source of rivers of mud or of debris long after they have erupted, and over the last three centuries they have killed more than a quarter of a million people.

volcanoes

▲ **MOUNT VESUVIUS**
This is the bustling Bay of Naples today, with the volcanic Mount Vesuvius looming on the skyline. On August 24, AD 79, the volcano erupted. A pyroclastic flow (a mass of gases and ash) raced down the slopes and buried the Roman towns of Pompeii and Herculaneum. The townsfolk were unprepared for the eruption, since Vesuvius had been dormant for centuries, and several thousand died, mostly from heat or choking. The next eruption may endanger as many as three million people.

▲ **POMPEII**
In Pompeii 2,000 people were buried by a layer of ash up to 100 ft (30 m) thick. The ash hardened into pumice, which preserved the shapes of the corpses. Plaster casts of the victims reveal their last moments.

▲ **INDONESIA**
Volcanic ash is not ash at all, but a fine powder made from tiny particles of rock and glass. After an eruption, it settles in layers and enriches the soil. The land surrounding the volcanoes of Indonesia is used for growing rice and other crops. The volcanoes lie beneath busy flight paths. Jets flying into a volcanic ash cloud from an eruption can have their engines badly damaged.

VOLCANO TIMELINE ►
Scientists rate the power of a volcanic eruption on a scale called the Volcanic Explosivity Index. Luckily, supervolcanoes that score 8 or more are rare. The last one took place about 74,000 years ago in Sumatra.

SCORING ON THE VOLCANIC EXPLOSIVITY INDEX

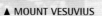

⑦	⑦	⑥	⑦
Crater Lake, Oregon c. 4895 BC	Kikai, Ryukyu Island, Japan c. 4350 BC	Santorini (Thera), Greece c. 1390 BC	Vesuvius, Italy AD 79

▲ GLOBAL SUNSCREEN

The explosion that rocked Mount Pinatubo was one of the largest eruptions of the 20th century. This satellite picture shows a vast plume of particles around the equator, 2 months after they were ejected 30 km (19 miles) into the atmosphere. They reflected the Sun's light and lowered the global temperature by 1°C (1.8°F).

▲ SEISMOMETER

A scientist sets up a seismograph to measure ground vibrations caused by volcanoes and earthquakes. Today seismologists monitor volcanoes that might erupt along busy flight paths, such as those over Alaska.

▲ PINATUBO

This strange scene was created by a shower of volcanic ash. In June 1991, Mount Pinatubo in the Philippines erupted in a titanic explosion, blowing more than 1.2 cu miles (5 km³) of rock and volcanic ash into the air. The debris then fell back to Earth in waves of hot ash. Heavy rains fell and created lahars: sludgy rivers of mud, wet ash, and rock. The lahars streamed down valleys at speeds of up to 40 mph (65 kph), burying houses and killing people.

▲ LAHAR (MUD FLOW)

Rainfall on Mount Pinatubo is very heavy from June to September. For 4 years after the 1991 eruption, lahars flowed without warning into nearby towns. In all, more than 100,000 people have lost their homes.

| Oraefajokull, Iceland 1362 | Tambora, Indonesia 1815 | Krakatau, Indonesia 1883 | Katmai (Novarupta), Alaska 1912 | Mount St. Helens, Washington 1980 | Pinatubo, Philippines 1991 |

EARTHQUAKES

Earthquakes commonly occur along Earth's tectonic plate boundaries, where there are faults. Faults are fractures that develop where tectonic activity is pushing the rock on one side past the rock on the other. But friction makes the rocks along the fault stick, and they become stressed. When the stress overcomes the friction, the rocks move suddenly, causing an earthquake. Its size depends on how much energy is released. There are three main faults: strike-slip, normal, and reverse or thrust faults.

EARTHQUAKE ZONES (FEATURED EARTHQUAKES)

QUAKE SITE	DATE	RICHTER SCALE	DEATHS
Alaska	1964	8.4	131
San Francisco	1906	8.3	500+
Duzce, Turkey	1999	7.2	260
Kobe, Japan	1995	6.9	5,500
Northridge, California	1994	6.7	51

▲ DUZCE, TURKEY (1999)
In 1999, an earthquake measuring 7.2 on the Richter Scale struck Turkey. Long faults make big earthquakes as they build up more stress along the length of the fault. The North Anatolian strike-slip fault in Turkey is more than 745 miles (1,200 km) long. Since 1939, there have been 11 large earthquakes on this fault.

▲ GRAND TETON MOUNTAINS, WYOMING
Some landforms are created by earthquake movements. The mountains of Grand Teton National Park in Wyoming were created by movement along a normal fault, where the rock is being pulled apart. Rocks along the east side of the Teton fault line move downward, leaving the opposing rock forming high mountains.

STRIKE–SLIP FAULT In strike-slip faults, ground movement is horizontal. In this right-lateral strike-slip, you would see the ground on the opposite side of the fault move to your right.

NORMAL FAULT In a normal fault, movement is caused by rock being pulled apart. The side above the fault line drops down—in this case in a near-vertical direction.

RICHTER SCALE
In 1935, American Charles Richter invented a scale for measuring the size, or magnitude, of earthquakes.

Generally not felt by people	Felt by few people	Felt by some: causes very little damage	Felt by most: causes little damage	Causes damaging shocks
1	**2**	**3**	**4**	**5**

◀ SEWARD, ALASKA
This fishing boat was hurled from the water by a Pacific-wide tsunami generated by the great Alaskan earthquake of 1964. People died as far away as Newport Beach, California. Most of the damage and lives lost from this earthquake were due to the effects of these giant water waves, created either by the movements of the ocean floor or by underwater landslides in nearby bays. Tsunamis can cross the ocean at speeds of up to 950 kph (600 mph) and reach fearsome heights of up to 30 m (100 ft) by the time they hit the coast.

▲ NORTHRIDGE, LOS ANGELES (1994)
Although the Northridge earthquake of 1994 was considered moderate, measuring only 6.7 on the Richter Scale, it was the most costly earthquake in US history. It was caused by movement on a thrust fault. Loss of life was minimized by strict building codes and the early morning hour of the quake.

REVERSE OR THRUST FAULT In reverse faults, caused by rocks being compressed, the side above the fault moves up. They are called thrust faults if, as here, the dip or angle of the fault is low.

tructive in
y populated
areas

Major earthquake: can cause serious damage

Great earthquake: can destroy towns over a wide area

7   8   9

▲ ALASKA, 1964
The 1964 Alaska earthquake was the second largest ever recorded, measuring 8.4 on the Richter Scale and lasting 4 minutes. On the modern earthquake measure, the Moment Magnitude Scale, it registered 9.2. The largest recorded earthquake (Richter 8.6, MM 9.5) struck Chile in 1960.

STUDYING EARTHQUAKES

What makes an earthquake destructive? The answer lies in the seismic shockwaves it sends out. There are different types of waves. Surface waves ripple along Earth's surface. These waves cause the most damage. Other waves, known as body waves, travel through Earth's interior. Seismic waves can be detected far away by sensitive vibration recorders called seismographs. Seismologists—scientists who study earthquakes—are still learning about Earth's interior and how earthquakes occur. A better understanding of why and when earthquakes happen can help to save lives in the future.

P-WAVES AND S-WAVES

Earthquakes send two kinds of body wave: P (primary) and S (secondary). P-waves push and pull like an accordion. S-waves "waggle" from side to side, like a rope. Both waves take curving paths, because they are bent by the differing densities they pass through. S-waves do not pass through the outer core, because they cannot travel through a liquid. Seismologists know how fast the waves travel, and that P-waves are nearly twice as fast as S-waves. They use seismographs of body waves to find out where earthquakes have occurred.

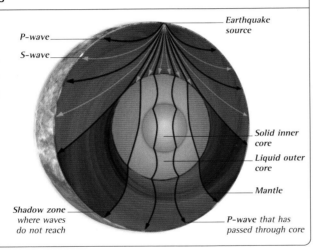

P-wave

S-wave

Earthquake source

Solid inner core

Liquid outer core

Mantle

Shadow zone where waves do not reach

P-wave that has passed through core

earthquakes

KOBE EARTHQUAKE ▶

On January 17, 1995, an earthquake hit the large city of Kobe in Japan. Earthquakes are common in Japan, which lies near the boundary between 3 tectonic plates. But the Kobe region had shown few warning tremors, and the city was unprepared. For example, some districts were built on soft, wet sand instead of rock. When wet sand is shaken violently, it flows like a liquid. At Kobe, about 100,000 buildings collapsed and 5,500 people died.

PREDICTING EARTHQUAKES

Dragon's head

ANCIENT CHINESE SEISMOGRAPH

In AD 132, the Chinese philosopher Chang Heng invented an earthquake detector. It was a large vase with 8 dragons' heads attached. Each dragon held a ball in its jaws, and beneath each head sat a cup in the shape of a toad with its mouth open. Any earthquake within a range of about 400 miles (640 km) would cause a ball to fall into a cup. The direction of the quake determined which ball would fall, so rescue parties would know where to go.

Clock triggered by sprung weight

PALMIERI'S SEISMOGRAPH

Luigi Palmieri tested this seismograph on Mount Vesuvius in Italy in 1865. It was rather complicated. U-tubes filled with mercury recorded horizontal vibrations. A weight hung on a spring recorded vertical vibrations. The sprung weight also triggered various clocks, which recorded the time and duration of vibrations.

◀ TURKEY EARTHQUAKE
This picture shows the extensive damage caused by an earthquake that struck the Turkish town of Duzce on November 12, 1999. Three months earlier, another earthquake had struck the nearby city of Izmit, killing 18,000 people. Turkey sits on a major fault in the Earth's crust. Each new tremor releases stress along a part of the fault. Seismologists believe that Ankara, the Turkish capital, will be hit before 2030.

5-SECOND UNITS

▲ KOBE SEISMOGRAM
This is a seismogram of the 1995 Kobe earthquake. The horizontal scale records time: the gap between each vertical line represents 5 seconds. The zigzag line shows how much the ground is moving, measured in millimeters against the vertical scale. The small zigzags at the left are a jumble of secondary and surface waves. The longest ones are all surface waves, taking up a total of about 20 seconds. These are the waves that caused most of the damage on the ground.

Earthquake epicenter

Colored bands show 4 in (10 cm) of ground movement

OBSERVATORY
Modern seismographs are based around the mechanism of a pendulum—a heavy weight on a spring hanging from a support. During an earthquake, everything shakes except the pendulum. In early seismographs, a pencil attached to the stationary weight drew zigzags on a rotating drum of paper, as the paper moved with the vibrations. The zigzags showed how much the ground was shaking. Today's readings are taken with more sophisticated electronic instruments.

SATELLITE IMAGE OF EARTHQUAKE ▲
A colored satellite radar picture shows an earthquake zone in California, in 1999. The colored bands are contours, each indicating 4 in (10 cm) of ground displacement, increasing toward the fault (upper center). The earthquake measured 7.1 on the Richter Scale. Radar measurements were taken before and after the event by a European Remote Sensing (ERS-2) satellite and the information was then incorporated into this image.

SAN ANDREAS FAULT

The San Andreas Fault in western California is probably the best-studied fault in the world. It is part of a boundary between two tectonic plates, and frequent earthquakes have been shaking the region for nearly 30 million years. The fault came to scientists' attention after 1906, when a major earthquake left San Francisco in ruins and hundreds of people dead. Since then, more earthquakes along the fault have claimed lives. But progress has been made, too, in designing stronger buildings, so that if—or when—the next "Big One" hits California, people will be better prepared.

FAULT LINE

The fault runs along coastal California for about 800 miles (1,300 km). Two plates are slipping jerkily past one another at about 1 in (25 mm) a year. Parts of the fault move little but often, causing frequent medium-sized tremors. Other sections can stick for up to 300 years, storing up energy. When these finally slip, the result is a major earthquake.

NORTH AMERICA

PACIFIC OCEAN

COASTAL CALIFORNIA (CLOSE-UP BELOW)

San Andreas Fault

San Francisco

Los Angeles

North American Plate *moving south*

Northern Pacific Plate *moving north*

CLOSE-UP OF FAULT

Fault line

▲ SAN ANDREAS FAULT
An aerial view shows the San Andreas Fault as an unmistakable scar across the land. If you stand at ground level, facing the fault, and look across, you can see that ridges and gullies no longer match up with each other. Whichever side you are on, the opposite landmarks lie to the right of where they used to be. Geologists call this type of fault a right-lateral, strike-slip fault.

▲ GREAT FIRE OF 1906
On April 18, 1906, a quake lasting about 45 seconds shook the northern end of the San Andreas Fault. In places the two sides of the fault moved up to 21 ft (6.4 m) past each other. In San Francisco, broken gas pipes started several fires among the city's old, wooden buildings. The blaze raged for three days. Firefighters were helpless because their water supplies had been disrupted.

earthquakes

HISTORY OF DESTRUCTION IN CALIFORNIA

1933 LONG BEACH QUAKE
Disaster struck California again in March 1933, in the form of an earthquake in Long Beach. Here, firefighters try to put out the resulting fire at the Dodge Tire Factory. Unlike the 1906 earthquake, which caused a fire that burned on and on and devastated San Francisco, the 1933 earthquake was quickly contained by the fire services.

1989 DAMAGED BRIDGES
The 1989 earthquake struck in a remote mountain range 60 miles (100 km) south of San Francisco, but the city did not escape damage. A double-deck highway collapsed, crushing the cars below. The quake killed more than 60 people, but the toll would have been higher without the lessons learned from earlier disasters.

◄ JAPANESE PAGODA

Cedar center pole is main support

Loose, clay- tiled roofs move if shaken

For more than 1,400 years the Japanese have built pagodas to survive earthquakes. Each story has heavy, clay-tiled roofs that are loosely attached to the building, and a strong cedar pole stands at the center. When hit by an earthquake, the whole building wobbles and sways with it instead of breaking apart. The pole bends in a wave motion, but the weight of the roofs acting against one another cancels out the waves and keeps the pole stable.

TRANSAMERICA BUILDING ►
San Francisco's tallest building, at 845 ft (258 m), is the Transamerica Pyramid, built in 1972. Its deep concrete-and-steel foundation, laid on rock, is designed to move with an earthquake, and the base stands on a network of stiltlike beams that can cope with twisting movements. During the 1989 earthquake, the top of the building swayed by as much as 12 in (30 cm) but it suffered no damage.

Pyramid shape allows light to street below, and also makes building more stable

LASER MONITORING OF GROUND MOVEMENT ▲
A researcher adjusts an experimental laser unit in the southern Sierra Nevada region of California, a highly active area where earthquakes are common. Lasers can detect movements in the Earth's surface as small as a hair's breadth. This type of system may one day serve as an early warning system of major earthquakes. Space scientists are also using the latest satellite technology to track ground movements on Earth.

MOUNTAIN BUILDING

Mountains form where tectonic plates converge. The largest peaks form where continental plates collide and stack up layers of Earth's crust. Plate boundaries can produce long mountain systems called ranges. The highest, most rugged ranges are usually the youngest – they are on active plates and are often still growing. Older ranges are lower, with gentler slopes. The key process in mountain building is the deformation of rock by folding (caused by rock layers bending under pressure) and faulting (when the pressure forces the rock to fracture). Volcanic activity, which is common where continental and oceanic plates converge, also plays a part.

WORLD'S MOUNTAIN RANGES

ALASKA RANGE, CARPATHIAN MOUNTAINS, URAL MOUNTAINS, ALPS, PYRENEES, ALTAI MOUNTAINS, ROCKY MOUNTAINS, APPALACHIAN MOUNTAINS, HIMALAYAS, ETHIOPIAN HIGHLANDS, ANDES, DRAKENSBERG, GREAT DIVIDING RANGE

HIGHEST MOUNTAINS	CONTINENT	HEIGHT
Everest (Sagarmatha)	Asia	29,035 ft (8,850 m)
Aconcagua	S America	22,835 ft (6,960 m)
Mount McKinley	N America	20,320 ft (6,195 m)
Kilimanjaro	Africa	19,340 ft (5,895 m)
Mount Elbrus	Europe	18,510 ft (5,640 m)

Mountain ridge formed from deformed sedimentary rock

MOUNT KAGBENI, HIMALAYAS ▶
The Himalayas are Earth's biggest mountain range. They include 96 of the world's 100 highest peaks, including the 29,030-ft (8,850-m) Mount Everest (Sagarmatha). They began forming when two continental plates collided 50 million years ago. The Indian Plate crumpled, pushing rock upward, and the range is still growing today.

mountains

Sedimentary layers are laid down

Second Z-shape fold begins to form

First fold become more deformed

SAND MODELS SHOWING TWO STAGES OF MOUNTAIN FORMATION

MODELING MOUNTAINS ▶
We can replicate one way in which mountains are formed using sand models. A paper sheet is slowly rolled underneath layers of colored sand. The paper creates friction under the sand, and folds start to develop. The more the paper is moved, the more folds are formed. Eventually, when the compressed rock cannot fold any more it fractures, creating fault lines. The final set of folds represents the newest mountain ranges.

Simple deformation of sedimentary rock

Foothills

Rocks fracture (fault) under pressure

Fold mountains created by repeated faulting and folding

◄ SIERRA NEVADA
The 350-mile (565-km) long Sierra Nevada range, which lies inland from the California coast, was formed by volcanic activity. As the Pacific Plate converged with the North American Plate and sank below it, rising magma was forced into the Earth's crust. The magma pushed up through the crust and cooled into a belt of granite. Faults tilted the range to the west, creating the present Sierra Nevada.

Granite cools very slowly, allowing the crystals inside to grow large enough to be easily seen

BANDED GRANITE ►
Granite rock makes up the backbone of the Sierra Nevada range. After a period of volcanic activity that ended about 80 million years ago, millions of years of glacial uplift and erosion wore away other volcanic rock, exposing the granitic core of the range and forming scenic features such as the Yosemite Valley.

◄ CHUGACH
The Chugach mountains follow the coastline of southern Alaska for 370 miles (600 km). As the Pacific Plate sank beneath the North American Plate, sedimentary rock was scraped off the sinking oceanic plate, folded and heaped up, and added onto the western edge of the American continent.

Ammonite fossils over 180 million years old

SEASHELLS IN ROCK ►
Geologists study fossils to learn how rocks formed. Ancient seashells in mountains show that these rocks came from the seabed. Fossils of sea life are found at high elevations in most mountain ranges. Fine-grained sedimentary rocks are one of the best types for preserving fossils.

Young peaks are still rising

Ancient slopes have been leveled by erosion

MOUNTAIN WEATHER CONDITIONS

▲ MOUNT ST. ELIAS, ALASKA
Mount St. Elias on the southern coast of Alaska rises to 18,010 ft (5,490 m) from sea level. This spectacular mountain was created by tectonic activity in the last few million years. It is still growing today, and rapidly moving glaciers erode the peak as it rises.

▲ APPALACHIANS
Formed before North America and Europe separated, the Appalachians in the eastern US are among the world's oldest mountains. Several hundred million years ago they were a range of high, pointed peaks, but constant erosion has worn them down to gentle slopes.

Great mountain ranges have a significant effect on the local climate. For example, the Andes mountains in South America create a massive barrier to moisture-laden winds blowing west. The peaks push up the air, which then drops its rain on the eastern slopes. Meanwhile, the western slopes are left dry. Similarly, the Himalayas cause monsoon winds to drop rain on the southern foothills; some villages in northeast India have an annual rainfall of more than 35 ft (11 m).

LANDSLIDES

A landslide is the sudden downward sliding of a mass of unstable material such as rock or soil. It is just one of the ways that a large mass of land material can move. In this case, it moves under the influence of gravity. A mass becomes unstable when it slopes too steeply, absorbs too much water, or is changed by the effects of weathering and erosion. Landslides can be triggered by natural events, such as earthquakes, or by human activities, such as road construction or quarrying. Some mass movements are so slow that they are barely noticeable, while others occur with deadly speed, sweeping over homes and people.

ROCKSLIDE ▶

Rockslides, common in high mountain ranges, occur when the angle of a slope is too great for the layers of rock to hold together. A slope may become unstable in spring after melted snow seeps into the rock, or when river water has eroded rock at the base. Water makes the natural boundaries between the different rock layers more slippery. The friction between the layers decreases and the upper layers begin to slide.

Soil creep is imperceptible—the topsoil moves downhill ³⁄₈ in (10 mm) a year

Slumping occurs when large slabs slip down vertically

Debris flow is likely when rain soaks a previously dry area, turning everything to mud

Rockfalls are the free movement of frost- or rain-loosened rock pieces

Bent telephone poles indicate soil creep

◀ LANDSLIDE TYPES
Geologists describe mass movements according to material, type of motion, and speed. Soil creep describes how minute shifts among soil particles cause slow movement. Slumping is a faster movement in which slices of land slip down a concave slope. In a debris flow, a water-soaked mass of rocks or soil moves fast like a liquid. Rockfalls, caused by rock weathering, are rapid and direct.

▲ MOUNT HUASCARÁN: LANDSCAPE BEFORE LANDSLIDE
Mass movements can travel unbelievably quickly. This picture of Mount Huascarán in the Peruvian Andes shows the scene before an earthquake struck on May 31,1970. The tremor dislodged a small amount of ice from the high, steep peak. The ice collapsed onto rocky slopes below. As the materials mingled, they gathered momentum, forming a massive debris avalanche.

▲ MOUNT HUASCARÁN: LANDSCAPE AFTER LANDSLIDE
This was the scene of devastation after the debris avalanche from Mount Huascarán. More than 65 million cubic yards (50 million m³) of rock, ice, and mud tumbled downhill at speeds up to 270 mph (435 kph). The tide of debris traveled 10 miles (16 km) downward, wiping out entire communities, including the village of Yungay, and killing more than 17,000 people.

▲ MUDSLIDE CAUSED BY HEAVY RAINS
Catastrophic mudslides such as this one in Caracas, Venezuela, in 1999, can occur in dry regions after sudden, heavy rainfall. Plant roots help to hold soil down, and there is a higher risk when farmers have cleared forested hillsides and left topsoil exposed. Because there is little vegetation to anchor the ground surface, water flushes the loose topsoil into stream gullies. The sloppy mixture of water and mud flows downhill, carrying away rocks, trees, and even cars and houses.

landslides

◄ MAKING SLOPES UNSTABLE
In 1995, a section of hillside slumped onto the California town of La Conchita. Luckily, no one was killed, although 9 houses were flattened. An investigation revealed that very high rains had left the hillside waterlogged and unstable. A law of landslides is that any slope will continue to settle until it finds its angle of repose—that is, the steepest angle at which the slope is stable. In La Conchita, the waterlogging had changed the hillside's angle of repose.

LANDSLIDES CAUSED BY SEAS AND RIVERS

The crashing of waves on this coastal cliff has eaten away at the rock at the base. The rock above the area of erosion now has no support. It becomes unstable and eventually topples. The eroded cliff edge is now getting dangerously close to the houses. Something similar happens with rivers, where constant steady erosion can make the riverbanks unstable. Brief but heavy rainfall can cause flash floods, causing steep riverbanks to collapse and destroy bridges and houses.

ROCKS

The rock that makes up the crust of Earth is constantly changing. Under the ground it is melted by heat and squeezed by pressures from deep within Earth. On the surface it is weathered by frost, wind, and water. Every form of rock can be classed in one of three groups— sedimentary, igneous, or metamorphic— depending on how it was formed and what changes it has undergone. Rock is changed or broken down by forces such as heat, pressure, and erosion, and turned by these forces into a new form of rock. This continual process is known as the rock cycle.

◄ YOSEMITE VALLEY
Every rock, no matter how hard, suffers weathering and erosion when it is exposed on the Earth's surface. This outcrop of jointed rock in Yosemite National Park is being splintered by "frost wedging," which occurs when water freezes and then expands, damaging the rock that surrounds it.

rocks

UPPER CRUST

SEDIMENTARY
Sediments deposited by water gradually build up in layers— layering is a feature of sediments and the rocks they form. Older, deeper layers are squeezed under the weight above them. They become compacted. The sediment has now become lithified: it is solid rock.

CONGLOMERATE
Formed from large pebbles, conglomerate was originally deposited by flowing water.

CHALK
Chalk is a form of soft limestone, made from tiny fossilised algae cells.

CRUST

IGNEOUS
Igneous rocks begin life as magma—rock heated in Earth's mantle until it is molten. When magma rises through the crust, it cools and crystallizes into new rock. The slower the process, the larger the crystal and the coarser the rock. Granite, for example, contains large mineral crystals that grew slowly.

PORPHYRY
Large crystals within a mass of finer grains are characteristic of this rock.

BASALT
Dark and fine-grained, basalt is the most common igneous rock in Earth's crust.

DEEPER CRUST

METAMORPHIC
Metamorphic rocks have been transformed from one form to another by heat or pressure, for example, by deep volcanic heat or by the stresses of mountain building. Some metamorphic rocks take on a flaky or layered structure when put under pressure. Others recrystallize altogether.

SLATE
Slate is produced by the metamorphosis of the sedimentary rock shale.

GNEISS
The metamorphis of silica-rich rocks, such as granite, creates this rock.

▲ EROSION

Erosion and weathering are a key part of the rock cycle. The exposed rock on these mountains is constantly being weathered by frost wedging and eroded by water. The smaller the rock fragment, the more easily it is moved. Rainwater washes the debris down the lower slopes. On many high mountain ranges, glaciers scour deep U-shaped valleys through the rock, carrying the loose debris downhill with them. When the debris is deposited over a large flat plain, as shown here, it is known as an alluvial fan.

◄ DEPOSITION

Every year, some 8,636 cu miles (36,000 km³) of water runs off the land into the oceans, carrying eroded material from surface rocks. Mud, silt, sand, and gravel are carried by flowing rivers. Along the way, some sediments are deposited on riverbeds and basins, such as these sediment plumes being deposited in the glacier-fed Peyto Lake in Alberta, Canada. Others end up on the margins of continents, where they build up to form sedimentary rock.

SHALE
This rock is a mixture of clay minerals with particles of quartz, feldspar, and mica.

SANDSTONE
Quartz makes up the majority of this largely medium-grained, common rock.

OBSIDIAN
When lava cools quickly it produces the glassy texture of rocks such as obsidian.

GABBRO
This is a hard rock that crystallizes underground over millions of years.

GRANITE
Known for its hardness, granite contains large crystals of quartz.

GARNET SCHIST
The term schist is used to describe a layered structure in metamorphic rock.

MIGMATITE
This rock is produced deep in the crust. It often contains bands of melted granite.

SIERRA NEVADA ►

Granite forms the foundation of many mountain ranges. Volcanic activity results in massive bodies of granite forming deep within the Earth's crust. Granite bodies larger than 40 sq miles (100 km²) are known as batholiths. Batholiths can be found in the Sierra Nevada and parts of the Rockies.

MINERALS AND CRYSTALS

More than 4,000 minerals are known. Some are very rare, while a small handful make up most of the rocks in Earth's crust. Geologists define a mineral as a naturally occurring inorganic solid, with atoms arranged in an orderly pattern. Minerals that grow in unconstrained environments develop regular forms and are called crystals. Minerals are mined from Earth for many uses. Some minerals occur as a single pure element, but most are compounds (a combination) of elements.

◄ GRANITE

Granite is an igneous rock that cools slowly underground. The slow cooling allows the mixture of minerals within to form large, easily visible crystals and give the rock its coarse-grained texture. Granite varies in color according to its mineral content: feldspar accounts for the pinkish tint, the grayish crystals are quartz, and the black specks are biotite.

BIOTITE

QUARTZ

FELDSPAR

Spring water is heated to about 160°F (70°C) before it emerges from the rocks

COPPER

◄ COPPER MINE, ARIZONA

Humans first worked copper into tools at least 8,000 years ago, and the metal is still much used today. It is an element that sometimes occurs freely as a metal, but is more usually found mixed with other elements in sulfide or oxide minerals. Rocks that contain enough metal-bearing minerals are known as ore. Copper is extracted from ores that contain as little as 0.5% metal, so large amounts of ore must be mined to produce it.

OTHER PRECIOUS METALS

SILVER

A rare and precious metal, silver was used in the earliest coins. Although it occurs in a native state, it is more common in compounds. Mexico, Peru, and South Africa contain important silver mines, although 75% of the silver produced each year is a by-product of the refining of gold, copper, zinc, and lead ores.

GOLD

Beautiful and easily worked, gold has been sought after since earliest times. The metal exists almost entirely in a native state. It is found in rock veins or streambeds, where it is washed after the weathering of gold-bearing rocks. Today, South Africa, Russia, and North America are the world's leading suppliers.

Pillowlike formations give Pammukale ("cotton castle") its name

Travertine stalactites form on the overhang of rock terraces

◄ **TRAVERTINE STALACTITES IN PAMMUKALE, TURKEY**
These great rock jaws were created by deposits of travertine (calcium carbonate) from a hot mineral spring. The hot spring water dissolves calcium carbonate, or calcite, from the limestone rocks through which it rises. The travertine deposits in Pammukale in Turkey cover an entire hillside. The stalactites—more usually found in caves—are formed when carbonate precipitates out as water drips down from a ceiling, or in this case, from an overhang.

LEAD

▲ **GALENA**
Most of the world's lead, and much of its silver, is extracted from galena. The mineral is an electrical conductor, and was used as the "crystal" in early crystal radio sets. Galena can be recognized by its heavy, silver-gray crystals, which are commonly cubic in shape. When struck with a hammer, the crystals cleave (split) neatly along regular planes.

Drusy quartz (fine crystals) inside a quartz rock cavity

minerals

DRUSY QUARTZ ▲
These small, clustered crystals are drusy quartz, which form when silica-rich groundwater trickles through bedrock and deposits crystals on the surfaces of rock cavities. This shows how minerals, given enough space, crystallize into regular shapes. All minerals try to form regular crystals, but are often prevented from doing so by their confined surroundings.

Raw diamond crystal in kimberlite rock

RAW DIAMOND ►
Diamond is the hardest mineral in the Earth's crust. It forms when deeply buried carbon is put under immense pressure at temperatures of up to 5,400°F (3,000°C). Diamonds are brought to the surface by explosive eruptions of a mantle rock, kimberlite. Raw diamond looks rather dull, and must be precisely cut to produce its distinctive sparkle.

ACID POLLUTION FROM MINING
Pyrite, a compound of sulfur and iron, is a widespread mineral that is commonly exposed during the mining of metal ores. Its metallic yellow color has earned it the nickname "fool's gold." The mining and processing of sulfide minerals is the source of most environmental concerns with metal extraction. When exposed to water or air, pyrite oxidizes (reacts with oxygen) to produce iron oxide and sulfuric acid. If the acid enters the environment, it can poison streams and lakes and kill plants.

PYRITE

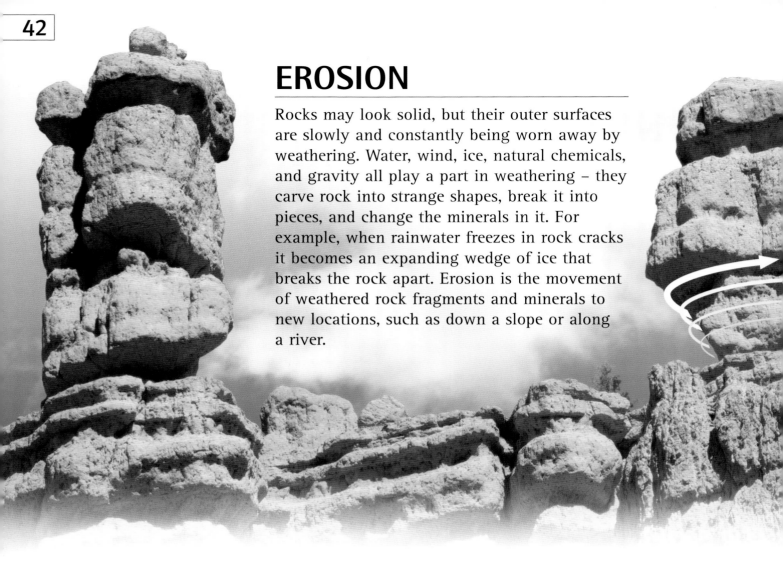

EROSION

Rocks may look solid, but their outer surfaces are slowly and constantly being worn away by weathering. Water, wind, ice, natural chemicals, and gravity all play a part in weathering – they carve rock into strange shapes, break it into pieces, and change the minerals in it. For example, when rainwater freezes in rock cracks it becomes an expanding wedge of ice that breaks the rock apart. Erosion is the movement of weathered rock fragments and minerals to new locations, such as down a slope or along a river.

Granite mountains in Yosemite stand 3,300 ft (1,000 m) tall

Sandstone pinnacles left by erosion

▲ EXFOLIATED GRANITE OUTCROP IN YOSEMITE
Outcrops of granite tower over the landscape of Yosemite National Park in California. The granite, a hard igneous rock, formed millions of years ago deep within Earth's crust. The rock overlying the granite has been eroded over the years. Freed from the pressure of the overlying rock, the granite begins to crack into layers like an onion. This is known as exfoliation. Water freezing in the cracks helps to separate the layers.

▲ HOODOO LANDSCAPE IN BRYCE CANYON
It is hard to believe that Bryce Canyon in Utah was once a solid plateau of sedimentary rock. Frosts have helped sculpt it into an eerie forest of towering hoodoos up to 200 ft (60 m) high. About 35 million years ago, the plateau was pushed up by forces in the Earth's crust. It split into rows of rock walls divided by deep cracks. The walls were weathered by frost into fins, jagged blades, and finally hoodoos. Rains running off the land flush away the rock fragments.

◄ HOODOOS

These hoodoos (rock pillars) are all that remain of the upper layers of a sedimentary rock plateau that has been weathered away. Cracks, opened up by rainwater and frost, have formed between each sedimentary layer in the hoodoos. The different rock layers weather away at different rates. The slender "necks" of the hoodoos are made of a soft rock, such as mudstone. This breaks up more rapidly than the harder rocks, such as limestone, above and below it.

erosion

Cracks between rock layers opened by frost wedging and chemical erosion

Slender neck of soft rock is worn away by wind action

CHEMICAL EROSION

ERODED LIMESTONE
Rainwater causes chemical erosion in limestone. The water reacts with carbon dioxide in the air to become weakly acidic. The acid reacts with the rock to dissolve the mineral calcite. The water then carries the calcite away. After a long period, this process of erosion etches deep grooves in the surface of the rock.

KARST LANDSCAPE IN CHINA
These outcrops of limestone in China have been eroded by acidic rainwater into a range of sharp blade-like rocks. Landscapes like this are known as karst terrain. The same process of chemical erosion is at work here as in the photograph on the left; it has simply reached a much more advanced stage.

Limestone arch formed by wave action on surrounding softer rock

◄ V-SHAPED VALLEY

Fast-flowing rivers carve V-shaped valleys as they rush down steep hills. At the Lower Falls on Yellowstone River in Wyoming, the rock walls are almost sheer: the water is downcutting (eroding its bed) faster than the walls are being weathered. The stream passes over different rocks on its way down: the waterfalls are caused by a shelf of hard rock that is resistant to erosion.

▲ COASTAL EROSION

Durdle Door is a natural rock arch on the Dorset coast in Great Britain. Set in a wall of two different limestones, the arch formed after the battering of sea waves eroded a panel of softer limestone. The cliffs on each side of the wall are made of even softer rocks. They have eroded much faster than the limestone, and the sea has worn away the coastline to make deep bays. The name of the arch comes originally from "thirl," an ancient English word meaning "pierced."

U-SHAPED VALLEY ►

Glaciers, or rivers of ice, create a trademark U-shaped valley in mountains. Boulders gripped in the moving bed of ice grind against the rock walls and erode them. This is a hanging valley: the end of one glacial valley opening halfway up the side of another, deeper valley that cuts across it.

ISLANDS

Islands are landmasses surrounded by water. They are found inland, surrounded by lakes and rivers, and offshore, surrounded by seas and oceans. Offshore islands fall into two broad types: continental and oceanic. The first kind lie on the shallow, flooded margins of continents and are simply outlying parts of the larger landmass. Oceanic islands are created from the seafloor, quite often in midocean, by volcanic and tectonic activity. Many islands are home to fascinating plants and animals that have arrived from elsewhere and changed in unique ways to suit their new land. The same is true of the humans who have populated the islands of the world.

FLOODED MARGINS
Some islands are simply non-submerged parts of nearby continents. During the last Ice Age, dry land connected the British Isles to western Europe. Mammoth, elk, and Stone Age human hunters used the land as a bridge. But the climate warmed, sea levels rose, and by about 8,000 years ago the islands were cut off.

DIVERGING PLATES
New Zealand originated on the east side of Australia. Starting about 85 million years ago, rifting and seafloor spreading opened and widened the Tasman Sea, carrying New Zealand east and separating it from Australia. Since this time, New Zealand has been an island with its own geological history.

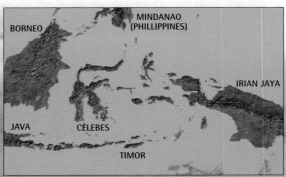

▲ INDONESIAN ARCHIPELAGO
Indonesia is the world's largest island group, or archipelago, spreading one-eighth the way around Earth. The western islands lie on a shelf off Southeast Asia, and the southern islands lie on another shelf off Australia. To the north and east, chains of active volcanic islands have been created over plate boundaries.

▼ INDONESIA'S ISLAND POPULATION
Not surprisingly, Indonesia's 235 million people reflect many different tribal groups and are spread out over 6,000 of the 17,000 islands. Today, many Indonesians are moving to find jobs in big cities. Three-quarters of the population now live on 6 main islands, including Sumatra and Java, where overcrowding is becoming a major problem.

BANDANAIRA ISLAND

STEPPING STONES

The islands of Indonesia and the Philippines (the busy island village of Cebu is shown here) provided some of the "stepping stones" used by humans spreading out from Asia across the Pacific Ocean. These voyagers made use of low sea levels to cross between neighboring islands, reaching Australia at least 60,000 years ago. For millions of years, plants and animals too have island-hopped on the wind and waves. Nowadays, travelling between the islands is relatively easy, as regular ferry services connect the island groups.

islands

◄ GALAPAGOS ISLANDS
The Galapagos are a chain of hot spot volcanic islands off the coast of South America produced from seafloor eruptions over the last 4 million years. As a result of their isolation, the Galapagos have unique animals and plants, including the marine iguana.

MARINE IGUANA ►
This reptile uses its flat tail to swim in the surf and is the world's only seaweed-eating lizard. English naturalist Charles Darwin visited the Galapagos islands in 1835, and the unique wildlife influenced his theory of evolution.

ALEUTIAN CHAIN, ALASKA
The Aleutians form a volcanic island arc around the northern Pacific Ocean. As the Pacific Plate drifts north into the North American Plate, its front edge sinks into the mantle. Magma rises from the mantle above the sinking plate to form volcanoes, which extend from midocean in the west to the Alaskan coast in the east.

BIRTH OF SURTSEY
Surtsey is one of Earth's youngest islands. It was born in November 1963, when a submarine volcano suddenly erupted off the coast of Iceland. For the next three-and-a-half years, basalt flooded from the seafloor to add to the volcano rising above the waves. Today the little island has an area of about 1 sq mile (2.5 km²).

Corals grow in shallow water fringing volcano

CORALS COLONIZE SHALLOWS

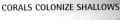

Ring-shaped coral reef grows and encloses peak

REEF APPEARS ABOVE SURFACE

Lagoon forms inside ring of coral as volcano is eroded

LAGOON COMPLETE

Volcanic peak within lagoon

Atoll is colonized by wind-blown or drifting plant seeds

Sandy beach formed from coral limestone

▲ FORMING A CORAL ATOLL
An atoll is a ring-shaped coral reef. It begins to form when skeleton-building corals grow in shallow water around the flanks of an ocean volcano. The corals build the reef up until it rises above the water. The volcano cone is eroded by wave action, and the crater is submerged, leaving just the ring of coral.

◄ ATOLL ANATOMY
Coral atolls form in the warm shallows of tropical seas, including the Caribbean, the western Pacific, and the Indian Ocean. The living corals are communities of small animals that trap food from the tides. Algae in the coral tissues help them build stony skeletons, which form the ring-shaped reef. Eventually the reef becomes an island, complete with coral sand beaches and colonizing plants and animals. The lagoons, protected from waves, provide calm harbors for shipping.

GLACIERS AND ICE SHEETS

Glaciers are permanent bodies of ice. They form on high mountains in many parts of the world, though the largest glaciers—ice sheets—cover the entire polar region. Glaciers flow slowly downhill, carving deep valleys in rock and calving (shedding) icebergs into the sea where they reach coasts. Today, ice covers one-tenth of the Earth's total surface, but at earlier times in the Earth's history it has covered an area three times bigger. Though glaciers grow and shrink with changing climates, they leave lasting evidence of their work. Many of our greatest mountain ranges were sculpted by the force of moving ice.

glaciers

▲ MARGERIE GLACIER, ALASKA
The most common form of glacier is a valley or alpine glacier. It usually flows down a mountain valley originally shaped by a stream. The tongue of moving ice scrapes away rock debris, or till, and bulldozes it into ridges and heaps. In time, the glacier changes the valley into a U-shape. A glacier may flow for just a few hundred yards or for hundreds of miles. Looking at a glacier, it is hard to get a sense of scale: these ice cliffs at the tip of the Margerie Glacier rise about 262 ft (80 m) above the water.

HOW A VALLEY GLACIER FORMS

A valley glacier usually starts flowing from a bowl-shaped hollow, known as a cirque. Here, two glaciers from neighboring cirques are merging into a single flow. Till (rock debris) is heaped up into deposits known as moraines. These deposits are found between the glaciers (medial moraine), at the sides (lateral moraine), and at the end or snout (terminal moraine). At lower altitudes, warmer temperatures melt the ice. The meltwater can form a lake, which is dammed by a wall formed at the end of the glacier.

Cirque: rock basin from which glacier flows

Nunataks: bedrock that projects through the ice

Rock avalanche

Crevasses: deep cracks in the ice

Lateral moraine: rock debris at side

Terminal moraine

Rocks plucked from valley floor

Medial moraine: rock debris trapped between glaciers

Meltwater stream trickles through glacier

Streams

▲ MALASPINA GLACIER, ALASKA
Where glaciers spill out of steep valleys into flat areas of land, they form a spreading tongue of ice known as a piedmont lobe. The world's largest piedmont lobe is the Malaspina Glacier, which covers more than 1,930 sq miles (5,000 km²) on the Gulf of Alaska. The outlet from which the glacier spills appears on this satellite image as a neck of ice. The neck looks narrow, but is actually 2.5 miles (4 km) wide. The S-shape to the left is the Agassiz Glacier.

▲ ICE SHEET MARGIN, GREENLAND
Icebergs litter the shores of Greenland. Four-fifths of the island is buried under a giant ice sheet measuring more than 656,000 sq miles (1.7 million km²). The ice sheet is domed, with two high peaks in the interior. Ice flows outwards from the domes to the coast, where the icebergs break away into the North Atlantic. Though vast, the Greenland ice sheet is dwarfed by the Antarctic ice sheet, which is nearly 8 times larger.

◄ ERRATIC BOULDER
As glaciers melt and retreat, they leave behind the rocks they once carried. Some are just pebbles, but others may weigh thousands of tons. These rocks are known as erratics. They can often be identified by their rock type, which is older or younger than the supporting rock, which gives scientists vital clues as to how glaciers moved. Glaciers have been known to transport erratics up to 500 miles (800 km).

Firn: compacted snow

Direction of wind

Ice shelf: where ice floats out to sea

Tabular icebergs are flat-topped

▲ HOW AN ICE CAP FORMS
An ice cap is a small ice sheet. It forms when moisture-laden winds drop snow on mountain slopes. In cold conditions the snow settles year after year. This buildup is called accumulation. As snowflakes are weighed down under new snowfall, they change into ice granules, then into a denser ice known as firn, and, after many years, into hard blue ice. Ice creeps downhill to coasts, where it melts or breaks up into icebergs. This loss of ice is called ablation.

ICEBERGS

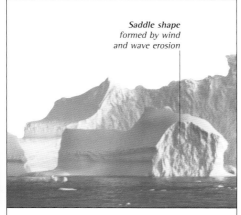

Saddle shape formed by wind and wave erosion

ARCTIC ICEBERG
Icebergs are floating chunks of freshwater ice that form when glaciers reach the sea. Arctic bergs are much smaller than Antarctic bergs and tend to be more irregular in shape. The oldest icebergs are blue, rather than white; their ice has formed over thousands of years and has had most of the air squeezed out of it.

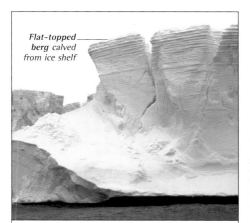

Flat-topped berg calved from ice shelf

ANTARCTIC ICEBERG
More than 90% of the world's icebergs are produced from the floating shelves of ice around Antarctica. The shelves are strained by water pressure until table-shaped icebergs calve (break away) into the water. It is a long journey from the glacier to the sea, and the ice in icebergs is an average of 5,000 years old.

ICEBERG SIZE
Only about seven-eighths of an iceberg's volume is visible above the water; the rest is hidden below the surface. Some are huge: in 1956, an iceberg larger than the country of Belgium calved from Antarctica. In 2002, an iceberg 550 ft (167 m) tall was sighted off the coast of Greenland.

SOIL

Plants: take in nutrients from humus

Humus: organic material, made up of decayed plant and animal matter

Topsoil: rich in humus and life-forms, such as earthworms

Subsoil: poor in humus, rich in minerals washed down from above

Weathered rock: high content of minerals from fragments of parent rock

Bedrock: unweathered parent rock, from which soil is ultimately formed

The top layer of the Earth's surface is made up of rock particles, minerals, air, water, and organic matter. Soil is produced when bedrock—the solid rock that lies under these particles—is weathered into tiny pieces and chemically altered by rainwater. The rate of weathering depends on rock type and climate, and there are many different kinds of soil. Soil's organic content, humus, comes from the plants, animals, and bacteria living within it. Soil is a life-support system. Plants depend on it, and we need it for growing food. But where humans do not manage soil carefully, it is quickly eroded or used up. It takes centuries to produce, and is not easily replaced.

e ▶▶ soil

◄ SOIL LAYERS
As soil forms, it settles into layers. Scientists class the layers in bands known as horizons, and together they make up a soil profile, which varies from one place to another. In this diagram of a mature forest soil, the upper horizons make up the topsoil, rich in humus, or organic matter. The subsoil below collects minerals washed out of the topsoil. At the very bottom lies the parent rock: the bedrock from which the soil is created by weathering.

▲ SOIL ENRICHERS
By burrowing through the ground and feeding on humus, earthworms help aerate the soil and mix up the mineral and organic content. In tropical grasslands, ground-dwelling termites play a similar role of transporting nutrients to the topsoil. Other soil enrichers include fungi and bacteria. They speed up the decay of plant and animal remains, turning them into humus, which is food for other organisms, such as trees.

▲ INTENSIVE FARMING
All our major food crops are grown in soil. As the world's population rises, the supply of good farming soil is running low. Crops take nutrients, such as nitrogen, out of soil, and farmers replace these by applying fertilizers. Meanwhile, agronomists—soil scientists—research ways of improving soil fertility, irrigation (watering), and drainage. They also look into producing new strains of higher-yielding crops that can produce more food from the same area.

▲ FOREST SOIL

In forested regions with a mild, moist climate, rainwater flushes clays and oxides from the topsoil. They build up in the subsoil, which is a rich red-brown color. Abundant forest vegetation adds to the humus content of the topsoil, which is highly acidic and pale. This kind of soil, called pedalfer, is common across the eastern United States and much of Europe. It makes good farmland.

FOREST SOIL
CLOSE-UP

▲ SOIL EROSION IN GAIZI VALLEY, CHINA

This valley in China has lost its soil through erosion. When soil is used repeatedly for growing crops, without a break between sowings, it becomes unstable. The removal of plant cover leaves it at the mercy of the wind and rain, which remove the soil and dump it in rivers. Across about one-third of the world's croplands, soil is being eroded faster than it is being replaced. The United States, for example, loses about 2.2 billion tons (2 billion tonnes) of topsoil each year.

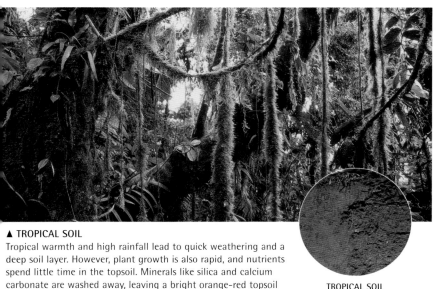

▲ TROPICAL SOIL

Tropical warmth and high rainfall lead to quick weathering and a deep soil layer. However, plant growth is also rapid, and nutrients spend little time in the topsoil. Minerals like silica and calcium carbonate are washed away, leaving a bright orange-red topsoil that is high in oxides and clay. Known as laterite, this soil can be farmed for only a year or two before it is exhausted.

TROPICAL SOIL
CLOSE-UP

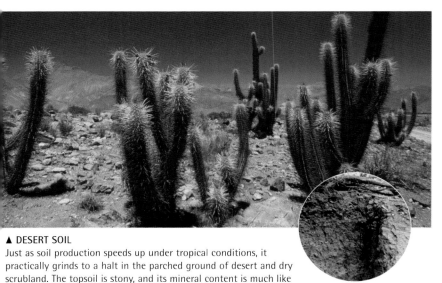

▲ DESERT SOIL

Just as soil production speeds up under tropical conditions, it practically grinds to a halt in the parched ground of desert and dry scrubland. The topsoil is stony, and its mineral content is much like that of the parent rock below. Water tends to dry off before it has the chance to sink in, and the subsoil contains a chalky layer of calcium carbonate left behind by the process of evaporation.

DESERT SOIL
CLOSE-UP

PROPERTIES OF CLAY

This clay-based soil has dried out and diminished in volume, creating cracks in the surface. Clay is made up of very fine mineral particles. It is an important ingredient in soil, storing up gases and minerals that are necessary for plant growth. However, too much clay in soil reduces its ability to soak up and store valuable water. Some clays swell when water is added to them and shrink when dry. Others are nonexpanding: they simply go soft when water is added. These are the clays used, for example, in the ceramics industry.

◀ SHANGHAI
Shanghai is China's key transportation center and one of the world's biggest seaports. The Huangpu River flows through its center before entering the Yangtze River nearby. At high tide, cargo ships can sail upriver from the ocean right into the city. The world's first cities grew up on the banks of rivers such as the Indus, Tigris, and Euphrates, where people depended on the water to irrigate their crops.

The Huangpu River is 70 miles (113 km) long

RIVERS

Rivers play a role in the water cycle by collecting rainfall that runs off the land and carrying it back to the oceans. On the way, they irrigate the land, supporting different ecosystems. Rivers leave their mark on the land, eroding rock and soil and carving deep valleys. When they reach the oceans, they deposit minerals and nutrients that help support marine life. Rivers provide various other benefits, from shipping lanes to fresh water, and their banks have been home to the world's greatest cities. But they also create danger in the form of floods.

rivers

Watershed separating drainage basins

Tributaries join the main stream

Drainage basin extends either side of river

ANATOMY OF A RIVER
A river collects runoff – rain or snow that runs off the land into rivers or seas rather than soaking in or evaporating – and transfers it back to the oceans. Along the length of the river valley, streams known as tributaries drain into the river.

WORLD'S LONGEST RIVERS

▲ YANGTZE
Flowing for 3,912 miles (6,300 km) through Tibet and China, the Yangtze is the largest river in Asia and the third largest in the world. Its source lies about 18,040 ft (5,500 m) above sea level in the Plateau of Tibet, and the river winds through deep valleys for much of its length.

▲ NILE
The Nile is the world's longest river. It starts in the mountains of East Africa and flows into Lake Victoria, before winding north through Sudan and Egypt to the Mediterranean on its 4,130-mile (6,650-km) journey. Heavy rains in Ethiopia cause the Nile to flood every summer.

▲ AMAZON
The Amazon is the world's second-longest river, flowing nearly 4,100 miles (6,400 km) across equatorial South America to the Atlantic Ocean. The river follows a winding course through the flat, low-lying Amazon rain forest. It floods every year, drowning the forest for months.

The Ganges delta is made up of thousands of silt-laden channels

FERTILE FARMLAND, NILE VALLEY ▲
Thousands of years ago, the Ancient Egyptian civilization flourished on the banks of the Nile. The river's annual flood deposited rich silt on the floodplains, creating a slim corridor of fertile land in the desert. Since 1970 the Aswan High Dam has controlled the floodwaters to make farming easier in the dry season. However, the dam stops the river from depositing silt, so farmers now have to use fertilizers to make their crops grow.

▲ GANGES DELTA
The Ganges River starts in the Himalayas and winds across India and Bangladesh for 1,560 miles (2,510 km). It is joined in Bangladesh by the Brahmaputra River, and they empty into the Bay of Bengal. Entering the bay, the current slows, and the water deposits sediment. Years of deposition have formed a vast, flat tongue of sediment known as a delta, over which the river splits into many separate streams.

TYPES OF RIVER

SEASONAL, CRETE
The Mallia River on the Greek island of Crete is swollen by springtime rain. Crete's rivers are especially short and flow over rocky hillsides. There is very little annual runoff to keep them flowing all year. In regions with a Mediterranean climate, rivers may dry up entirely during the long, hot summers.

EPHEMERAL, AUSTRALIA
A pool shrinking under the desert sun is all that remains of the Todd River in Australia's hot Northern Territory. It is a so-called ephemeral river—one that flows only occasionally. Once every year or so, brief and heavy rains cause the Todd to burst its banks, but the water soon evaporates or soaks into the ground.

PERENNIAL, US
Giant rivers like the Mississippi never stop. "Old Man River" flows 2,347 miles (3,780 km) from Lake Itasca, Minnesota, through the US to the Gulf of Mexico. It is the longest river in North America, draining an area of 1.83 million sq miles (4.76 million km²) that includes 31 US states and 2 Canadian provinces.

◄ THREE GORGES DAM, CHINA
China's Yangtze River floods regularly, killing thousands of people each year. In 1992 the Chinese government began building a dam across it. The Three Gorges Dam is due to be finished by 2009. It is intended to control the flooding, and also to provide a clean source of electricity.

▲ FLOODING IN BANGLADESH
Bangladesh lies on the delta of several large rivers, including the Ganges, Meghna, Surma, and Jamuna. The countryside is flat and low-lying, and the rivers shift their course every year. Devastating floods happen regularly, sweeping away animals and people. But the floods are not entirely unwelcome, since they bring rich silt that improves the soil and helps crops grow.

CAVES

Caves are spectacular natural spaces created out of rock by the action of water. For instance, the lapping of waves against a cliff can gradually erode (wear away) the rock face to create a cave. Caves also form when buried rock, usually limestone, is dissolved by groundwater—rainwater that has soaked into the land. Other rocks, such as sandstone, slowly collect groundwater like a sponge and store it. Groundwater is a precious freshwater resource. It feeds rivers and lakes during dry seasons, and supplies many homes, farms, and industries.

CAVE BATS ►
Caves offer bats a habitat for breeding and resting in large groups called colonies. In the tropics, bat colonies spend the day in a cave before flying out at dusk to hunt flying insects or feed on tree fruits. (By hunting at night, they avoid competing with birds for the same food resources.) In cooler regions, bats find less to eat as winter approaches, and many species find the stable temperature of a cave ideal for their long winter sleep.

HOW A STALACTITE FORMS ►
Groundwater is mildly acidic because it contains carbon dioxide captured from the air. As it flows through a layer of limestone, the acid dissolves calcite from it, creating the spaces that become caves. But when water drips from a cave ceiling, some of the water evaporates in the air. This makes the water release a tiny trace of calcite on the ceiling. Drip by drip, trace by trace, the calcite deposits build up into a stalactite.

Calcite deposits from dripping water form main body of stalactite

Drop of water at tip of stalactite

▲ CAVE PAINTINGS
Our prehistoric ancestors knew all about the caves in their territories, and made full use of them for shelter and defense from other humans and predatory animals. The earliest known art is in the form of paintings on the walls of caves. These beautiful bisonlike creatures are copies of originals found in the caves in Lascaux, in southern France. These animals were obviously important to our ancestors and were painted with great care.

◄ STALACTITES AND CAVE INTERIOR

Calcite deposits can turn a cave interior into a fantastical landscape. When calcium-rich water drips from stalactites, it leaves a trace of calcite on the floor directly below. These traces slowly build up into a mound called a stalagmite. A stalagmite may grow so tall that it merges with the stalactite above to form a complete column in an underground cave. It takes hundreds or even thousands of years to form large stalactites and stalagmites.

caves

Sinkhole allows water underground

Chimney is a near-vertical opening in rock

Gallery is a large underground chamber

Stalactite hangs down from the roof of the cave

Stalagmite rises from the floor of the cave

Impermeable layer through which water cannot pass

Underground lake

▲ CAVE CHARACTERISTICS

Limestone caves form during periods when the rock mass is soaked through with groundwater. Weakly acidic water flows into pockets and cracks in the rock, dissolving away calcite from roofs, walls, and floors alike. Horizontal cracks open out into flooded gallery caves linked together in complex systems. In time, the surrounding landscape changes. Rivers drain the caves, finding exits above deep layers of harder rock. But groundwater continues to filter through the caves, forming stalactites and stalagmites.

▲ UNDERWATER SPRINGS

An oasis survives in the desert, thanks to the water table. Below a certain depth, groundwater fills every available pore in rock or soil. The upper limit of this waterlogged zone is called the water table. Above that, there is a mixture of air and water. In a valley or a desert basin where the water table is near or even above the surface, groundwater is available as a spring, a well, or a lake.

▲ SINKHOLE COLLAPSE

When water creates limestone caves close to the ground surface, the cave roof may become so thin that it collapses without warning, forming a sinkhole. This huge hole opened up in an urban parking lot in Atlanta, Georgia in 1993; other sinkholes have been known to swallow whole houses. Regions that are heavily pitted with sinkholes are called karst landscapes. They are named after the Karst region of Slovenia in eastern Europe, where such terrain is common.

DESERTS

There are many different kinds of deserts. Those that are hot all year round are called hot deserts. They lie within 15-35 degrees north or south of the equator. Cold deserts are found farther north or south. They may be hot in summer but are cold and dry in winter. Rain-shadow deserts are dry because nearby mountains stop moist air from bringing rain to them. West coast deserts, swept by cold, dry ocean winds, are some of the driest places on Earth. All deserts have one feature in common: an annual rainfall of less than 16 in (400 mm).

◄ SAHARA

The Sahara is a hot desert, and one of the world's largest at 3.5 million sq miles (9 million km²). It is a landscape of rocky plains, basins, and plateaus, as well as sand seas. Today the Sahara is hot and dusty, but its climate used to be milder and moister. Fossils show that it was once a fertile land with rivers and lakes.

DESERTS		3.7% EARTH'S SURFACE
TYPE	AREA	PRINCIPAL LOCATIONS
Hot desert	77%	N Africa, Arabia, India
Cold desert	18%	C Asia
Rain-shadow	3.5%	Chile, California
West coast	1.5%	Namibia, Peru

Telson, or stinger,
contains venom

Pedipalps are
powerful pincers

◄ SCORPION

Scorpions are arachnids, relatives of spiders and mites. They survive in the desert by avoiding the daytime Sun. Some species hide under rocks, while others lurk in sandy burrows that they dig with their 8 legs. At night they come out to hunt for insects, lizards, and rodents. The cuticle, or outer skeleton, has a waxy coating that helps keep body fluids from drying out.

◄ CAMEL

Dromedary camels (with a single hump) are native to Arabia, but have been used in northern Africa since the days of Ancient Egypt. They helped traders ferry ivory, salt, and gold across the Sahara, and carried native tribes into desert battles. They can travel for up to two weeks without needing to drink, and, unlike sheep and cattle, they do not overgraze desert plants.

DESERT PLANT LIFE

STURT'S DESERT PEA
This plant is a flowering herb that grows in the deserts of central and southern Australia. The gray leaves are coated in fine, short hairs that trap water and keep the leaf surfaces damp. The seeds have a hard coating that protects them through long droughts, but when rain falls they rapidly sprout long roots.

PALM TREES
Desert peoples of Africa and Asia have grown the date palm for thousands of years, putting it to hundreds of uses. For example, they get food from its fruit, flowers, and pollen; alcohol from its sap; rope from the leaf fibers; lumber from the trunk; and charcoal from the date stones. The tree grows near oases, not in the desert.

CACTI
Superbly adapted to life in the American deserts, cacti grow in all shapes and sizes. The juicy stems swell up during rainy periods to hold water reserves for the dry months. Most cacti have spines in place of leaves (which would lose too much water). Spines also prevent animals from nibbling the stems and damaging them.

TAMARISK
These trees grow up to 10 ft (3 m) tall and thrive in the deserts of central Asia, even in very salty soils. The long roots tap into stored water deep below the ground, so the trees do not depend on rainfall. In long droughts, tamarisks simply shed the scalelike leaves on their slender branches and become inactive.

◄ DESERT RECLAMATION
Anything will grow in a desert if you use enough water. In these circular fields in New Mexico, pipes take water from deep beneath the desert's surface or from the Colorado River, and sprinkle it over crops. But careless irrigation can be destructive. It may pollute rivers and poison native desert plants with salty minerals.

ATACAMA DESERT ►
The Atacama Desert on the west coast of South America is both a rain-shadow desert and a west coast desert. The mountain ranges of the Andes to the east force moist air to shed its rain before reaching it. Any ocean winds that do reach the desert from the west contain little moisture because they blow in over cold water. The Atacama has large deposits of salt, which accumulate in basins called salars.

deserts

Plateau: a large flat area with steep cliffs

Wadi: a dry gully eroded by flash floods

Mesa: a small, separate plateau

DESERT FEATURES ►
Loose sand is heaped into straight, curving, or pyramidal dunes by the wind. Water erodes rocky hills to create flat tables. Torrents from brief rainfall carve gullies in rock and spread fans of sediment in low basins. Water either evaporates from basins or soaks away. Oases are islands of life that form in low-lying areas where water is found at or near the surface.

Inselberg: an island of erosion-resistant rock

Crescent dunes formed by wind

Wind direction affects shape of dune formation

Oasis: water source that supports plantlife

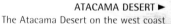

TROPICAL FORESTS

Tropical forests are found in lands on or near the equator, where the Sun's heat is at its greatest, and warm, rising air drops heavy rainfall. There are many kinds of tropical forests. Some are hot, with long, dry seasons. Others are cloaked in cool mist on high mountains. The best known are the lowland rain forests, which are permanently warm and wet. Although tropical forest covers less than three percent of the Earth's surface, it harbors more plant and animal life than any other biome on Earth.

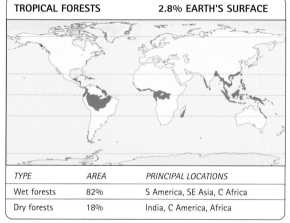

TROPICAL FORESTS		2.8% EARTH'S SURFACE
TYPE	AREA	PRINCIPAL LOCATIONS
Wet forests	82%	S America, SE Asia, C Africa
Dry forests	18%	India, C America, Africa

WET FOREST ▶

In a lowland rain forest, thousands of plant species live jumbled together and tend to form several layers. The treetop "canopy" takes most of the light, and the layers grow steadily darker, cooler, and damper toward the shady forest floor. Leaves are large, waxy, and thick, with "drip tips"—drooping, pointed ends that shed water easily to avoid unhealthy waterlogging.

◀ DRY FOREST

In a monsoon forest, warm summer winds blow in off the ocean, bringing heavy rain. Cool, dry winds blow the other way during winter, creating a dry season. A monsoon forest has a lower, more open canopy than a rain forest, allowing light to reach the floor, which becomes thick and junglelike.

tropical forests

▲ EVERGREEN HOLLY

While some of the upper-canopy trees in a monsoon forest shed their leaves during the dry season, trees and shrubs such as holly, in the lower layers, usually keep their foliage. This makes these forests semievergreen.

FLOODED FORESTS OF THE AMAZON

Tropical forests become flooded when rivers burst their banks after a high rainfall. In parts of the Amazon, trees spend up to 7 months of the year standing in water that may be tens of yards deep. Buttress roots act like props around the base of the trunk to help stop them from falling. The deep waterways of the Amazon are home to a freshwater dolphin, known locally as the boto. It has a long slim beak, which it uses to probe for food in the mud on the riverbed. It feeds on crabs, river turtles, and catfish.

EMERGENT
The tallest rain-forest trees have straight trunks with branches only at the crown (top). These giant trees are known as "emergents" because their crowns "emerge" from the canopy into full light.

Toucan bill is hollow with sharp, sawlike edges for holding fruit

TOCO TOUCAN ▶
The toucan is at home in the rain forest, where it nests in tree holes and uses its huge bill to crush and chop fruits. While flying, the toucan often drops fruits to the floor. Many of these grow into new trees, increasing the toucan's food supply.

CANOPY
At heights of 66–98 ft (20–30 m), the crowns of tall trees spread out until they almost touch, fitting together like a jigsaw, forming an almost unbroken leafy canopy that traps most of the sunlight.

◀ SQUIRREL MONKEY
At home in the high canopy of Central and South American rain forests, squirrel monkeys live in large groups, numbering 50 or more. They feed on anything from fruit to spiders and young birds in nests.

BROMELIAD ▶
Bromeliads are epiphytes—plants that are not rooted in the soil but which grow perched on tree branches. Their roots take up moisture and nutrients from the tree or from the air itself.

Long leaves collect rainwater

UNDERSTORY
Smaller trees often form a lower canopy about 50 ft (15 m) above the ground, filtering out much of the light, so that in some forests only 2–3% of the available light reaches the forest floor.

◀ SPINY DEVIL KATYDID
Katydids are some of the noisiest rain-forest insects. The males rasp their wings together to "sing" loudly for a mate. Many katydids eat flowers and leaves, though some attack tiny insects trapped in water pools in plants. In turn, katydids are prey for birds, bats, and monkeys. They tend to be green and leaf-shaped, and perch motionless to avoid being eaten.

Large eyes help to spot prey and judge attack distances

Spines on the body discourage birds or monkeys from making the katydid their next meal

FOREST FLOOR
The dark forest floor consists of tree roots covered in leaf litter, which is recycled by billions of ants and termites. Fungi in the soil also convert the debris into nutrients, which are absorbed by the roots.

GABOON VIPER ▶
Snakes rely on the Sun's heat to warm their bodies, so they thrive in tropical forests. This Gaboon viper lives on the African rain-forest floor. It has the longest fangs of any snake, measuring up to 2 in (50 mm).

Skin pattern acts as camouflage on the forest floor

Leaves form pitchers (jugs) that attract flies and other insects by exuding a strong-smelling nectar

PITCHER PLANT ▶
Where rain-forest soils are poor, plants find nutrients in unusual ways. A pitcher plant traps and digests insects inside its fluid-filled pitcher.

TEMPERATE FORESTS

Temperate forests grow where temperature, rainfall, and hours of sunlight change a lot through the year. The boreal, or coniferous, forest is a vast belt around the northern hemisphere, made up of evergreen, cone-bearing trees. Broadleaf deciduous forests flourish in cool, wet winters and mild, moist summers. These trees, which include oak and beech, shed their leaves in winter to conserve energy. Mediterranean forests are characterised by the dry summers and mild winters typical of the Mediterranean. Temperate rain forest often grows beside mountains on mild, rainy coasts.

TEMPERATE FORESTS		4.7% EARTH'S SURFACE
TYPE	AREA	PRINCIPAL LOCATIONS
Deciduous	56%	Canada, Siberia
Coniferous	32%	Tasmania, W Europe
Mediterranean	11%	Mediterranean, California
Rain forest	1%	NW US, Chile, NZ, Japan

temperate forests

▲ BROWN BEAR
The long temperate winters drive many mammals into hibernation. This is a deep sleep in which the heartbeat slows down and the body uses very little energy. The brown bear hibernates for up to 7 months each year in a den among tree roots or in a cave. It does not wake to feed, but survives on body fat stored up in the fall. The female even gives birth in her den.

▲ GRAY WOLF
The gray wolf was once widespread in North America, Europe, and Asia. Fear of this predator drove settlers to destroy all but a few wolf packs, which lived deep in the northern forests, mountains, and tundra. Today these habitats are the wolf's stronghold. Wolves live in packs. Hunting together, they bring down animals as large as deer and moose, then share the kill.

▲ CONIFEROUS PINES IN SNOW
Cone-bearing trees, known as conifers, are most common in cool, temperate zones and on mountain slopes, where their short branches help them to shed snow and rain easily. The densely growing boreal forests contain just a few, very hardy conifer species. Their leaves are needle-shaped and have a waxy surface, so that they lose little water. Since they remain on the tree all year round, the needles start soaking up the Sun's warmth as early as possible in spring. Their dark color also helps them absorb sunlight.

▲ DOUGLAS FIR CONE
These are cones of the Douglas fir, native to western North America. A conifer produces two kinds of cone on the same tree: male cones, which bear pollen, and female cones, which contain eggs. Blown by the wind, some of the pollen reaches the female cones and fertilizes the eggs, which produce seeds. After ripening, the seeds scatter, falling to the ground and becoming embedded in the soil to produce new growth.

FOREST FIRES

For millions of years, fire has played a role in the ecology of forests. It changes the mix of plant and animal species, and returns nutrients such as nitrogen to the soil. Some trees, such as the Douglas fir, grow thick bark as they mature, which helps them survive fire. Today, human activities are disturbing natural burning patterns, sometimes leading to uncontrollable fires that can destroy forests.

▲ DECIDUOUS FOREST

Each year, the onset of cold fall weather and the drop in light levels cause deciduous trees to shed their leaves. Fresh leaves grow in spring to continue the role of photosynthesis—using the Sun's energy to turn carbon dioxide and water into sugars for food. Meanwhile, fallen leaves create a carpet of decaying organic matter that nourishes plants, fungi, and insects such as beetles. Open deciduous woodlands contain a floor cover of shrubs such as hazel.

▲ CROCUSES

A crocus times its flowering to make the most of changing conditions in deciduous woodland. In winter and summer it stores food in its corm, an underground bulblike structure. It typically flowers in early spring, when the temperature rises but tree branches are still bare, letting the Sun's rays through to warm the forest floor. Some crocuses flower in the fall, after the trees have shed their leaves.

▲ TEMPERATE RAIN FOREST

On certain shores, moist winds from the ocean shed heavy rain on coastal forests. A mild climate, high humidity, and heavy rainfall make ideal growth conditions for some of the world's largest trees, such as the 328-ft (100-m) high redwoods of the American Pacific Northwest.

▲ FERNS

Temperate rain forests are thick with climbers, moss, and understory plants. Ferns thrive in warm, wet forests. Their leaves first appear as croziers—shoots shaped like a shepherd's crook that gradually unfurl. The leaves shed tiny cells called spores, which produce new plants.

GRASSLANDS

Before it was reduced by the spread of crop farming and ranching, grassland covered as much as two-fifths of Earth's land surface. It is found from the cold northern plains to the hot tropics, and takes many forms, which all share certain features. For example, the annual rainfall usually lies between 10 and 31 in (250–800 mm). This is too low for trees to take root, too high for desert to take over, but ideal for nonwoody, flowering plants such as grasses. Many grasses grow best if they are regularly burned.

GRASSLANDS		6% EARTH'S SURFACE
TYPE	AREA	PRINCIPAL LOCATIONS
Temperate	67%	Australia, Russia, China, N America
Tropical	33%	Sub-Saharan Africa, Brazil, Mexico

▼ SERENGETI SAVANNA

In the Serengeti National Park in Tanzania, East Africa, mammals graze the lightly wooded, tropical grassland known as savanna. The largest, such as the elephant and buffalo, graze and trample the longest grasses, making way for wildebeest and zebra, which graze shorter grasses. Tiny, delicate gazelles graze the short stems. The grazers migrate from one waterhole to another as the seasons change, followed by big cats and other predators.

LIFE IN THE TROPICAL GRASSLANDS

TERMITE MOUND
Termites are insects that live in colonies. Many tropical grassland species build soil mounds, an activity that brings nutrients up to the surface vegetation. Termites eat dung, grass, and organic particles in soil, and are among the few animals that can digest cellulose (a tough substance in plant cells).

SABLE ANTELOPE
Feeding out in the open is dangerous: grazers must keep watch for hyenas, lions, and leopards. Hoofed mammals of the savanna have evolved lean, light limbs for fleeing fast, and some—like the sable antelope—have sharp horns, too, to defend themselves as a last resort if there is nowhere left to run.

grasslands

CHEETAH ▶
The cheetah is the world's fastest land animal, sprinting at up to 68 mph (110 kph) in short bursts while chasing small antelope prey. This makes it unlike any other large African predator. But although special skills bring advantages, they also create problems. The cheetah has evolved into such an open-grassland expert that it cannot hunt in any other habitat type. And as grassland disappears under the plow, the cheetah has become rare.

▼ NORTH AMERICAN PRAIRIE
Temperate grassland in North America is called prairie. Varying climate conditions across the continent create three prairie types: tallgrass in the east, mixed-grass on the Great Plains, and shortgrass to the drier west and south. In the past, fires (some started by lightning, others deliberately by Native Americans) burned off the dry grasses each year, promoting fresh growth. Around 79% of the original prairie has been built on or converted to farmland.

LIFE IN THE TEMPERATE GRASSLANDS

WHEAT
More than half a billion tons of wheat are grown in the world each year, and Canada and the United States are among the top 6 producing countries. The crop is grown upon former prairie lands, where the soil is now so exhausted that farmers have to fertilize it heavily every year in order to reap a satisfactory harvest.

PRAIRIE DOGS
These plump, burrowing rodents of the plains grow up to 12 in (30 cm) long, and live in large warrens known as towns. The towns have sleeping chambers, food stores, and emergency exits for escape from their main predators, which are ferrets or snakes. Their name comes from their habit of giving a sharp, repeated bark to warn one another of danger.

ENDANGERED BISON ►
The plains bison is a wild American relative of domestic cattle. The powerful bulls weigh up to a ton. Bison herds once ranged across North America in their tens of millions, but during the 1800s white settlers slaughtered the animals for their hides and meat. Bison were also killed in order to starve the Plains Indians, and by the 1880s were nearly extinct. Today, after more than a century of protection, their future is secure.

DUSTBOWL IN AMERICAN MIDWEST ►
High winds on the Great Plains between 1935 and 1938 blew away so much soil that a vast area of 15.6 million sq miles (40 million km²) was left a wasteland. Americans called it the Dustbowl. The damage had started in the 1860s, when settlers grew the wrong kind of wheat and allowed cattle to overgraze the plains. Root systems were gradually destroyed, so that the soil was easily stripped away when the storms struck.

Clouds of dust blotted out the Sun and swamped farms during the storms of the 1930s

WETLANDS

Wetlands include any site where the soil is waterlogged part or all of the time. They comprise fresh and saltwater habitats, from bogs and swamps to coastal mangrove forests. Wetlands are vital refuges for animals, help cleanse polluted waterways, and buffer the land against extreme weather, acting like a big sponge to control floods. But their dependence on water makes them fragile, and because their importance is often ignored, wetlands are today some of the most threatened of all the Earth's biomes.

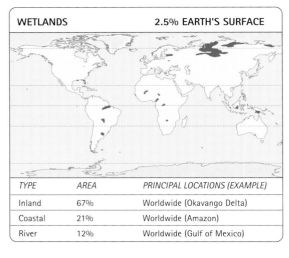

WETLANDS		2.5% EARTH'S SURFACE
TYPE	*AREA*	*PRINCIPAL LOCATIONS (EXAMPLE)*
Inland	67%	Worldwide (Okavango Delta)
Coastal	21%	Worldwide (Amazon)
River	12%	Worldwide (Gulf of Mexico)

Wings are capable of carrying them great distances

DRAGONFLY ▲
Dragonflies are fierce hunters with superb vision. They are found near wetlands because they depend on water for part of their life cycle. The nymph (larva) spends up to 5 years underwater.

▲ RIVER
Rivers are continually changing. For example, silt carried in the water erodes the banks in places where the current is strong, but is deposited in slow-flowing sections to form banks. Together, erosion and deposition alter a river's course. Heavy flooding creates temporary wetlands on the floodplains. These nourish the soil and also attract flocks of migrant birds.

▲ GRAY HERON
The gray heron is one of the top predators in the food web of a European river. (It is replaced in North America by the great blue heron.) The heron hunts fish and frogs, sometimes by standing in wait, but also by stalking through shallows, its neck hunched in readiness to strike with its long, stabbing bill. Other top river predators include the otter, mink, and, in slow rivers, pike.

▲ INLAND WETLAND, NORTH CAROLINA
In North America, bald cypress and water tupelo are two trees adapted to standing in water for part or all of the year. They survive swamp life by sending out "knees"— gnarled stilt-like support roots around the base of the trunk. The knees are thought to stabilize the tree and also to take up oxygen. Animals of the swamps include wood duck, egrets, and black bears.

THE ARAL SEA

The Aral Sea, located in Uzbekistan and Kazakhstan, was once the world's fourth largest inland sea, with an area the size of Southern California. About 40 years ago, its level started dropping, when vast amounts of water were diverted for cotton irrigation to satisfy Soviet agricultural production requirements. The sea has shrunk so much that its surface area has more than halved, its volume has decreased by 75%, and parts of the sea-bed have become salty desert. If present trends continue, the Aral Sea will disappear altogether.

e ►►
wetlands

High-set eyes and nostrils allow alligator to see and breathe while submerged

Hinged, bony plates strengthen the scales and provide protection

ALLIGATOR ►
The American alligator plays an important role in wetland ecosystems of the southeastern United States. To survive the dry season, when it is inactive, an alligator digs itself a watery hole in the mud. Other wetland creatures, from frogs and fish to turtles, hide in these "gator holes" until the rains return to swell their usual habitat.

▲ MOSQUITO
Like the dragonfly, the mosquito spends the larval stage of its life cycle in stagnant water. To nourish the eggs in her abdomen before laying them, the female stabs the skin of another animal, such as a frog, a bird, or a mammal, and draws off a meal of blood. Some mosquito species spread a dangerous disease called malaria, which is the world's number one natural killer.

▲ COASTAL WETLAND, FLORIDA EVERGLADES
The Everglades lies in subtropical Florida. At its heart lies a vast peatland, created by the slow buildup of dead plants. After rain, fresh water drifts south through a mosaic of grassy marshes and "hammocks" (tree islands), which give way farther south to coastal salt marshes and mangrove swamps. The region is threatened today by drainage for agriculture and domestic use.

▲ MANATEE
The West Indian manatee is an aquatic mammal that feeds on water plants. Swimming with the use of broad flippers and a spadelike tail, it cruises the mangrove swamps and rivers of the Gulf of Mexico, grazing heavily on sea grasses and other water plants. Feeding for up to 8 hours daily, the manatee helps keep coastal wetlands free of choking water weeds.

THE ARCTIC

Fringing the top of the northern continents lies a vast, treeless plain dotted with lakes: the Arctic tundra. The Arctic region receives little sunlight. Winters are long and dark, with little snowfall, and the soil is deep-frozen all year. Plants need to be tough and low-growing, and they include mosses and lichens. North of the tundra lies the Arctic Ocean. The waters surrounding the North Pole are covered with sea ice, which spreads and retreats with the changing seasons. Though the climate is hostile, the Arctic region is rich in insect, mammal, fish, and bird life.

polar regions

◄ THE ARCTIC
The Arctic biome effectively starts north of the treeline—the line beyond which trees cannot grow. It is defined by the Arctic Circle at latitude 66' 30" North. The Arctic Ocean, at 5.5 million sq miles (14 million km²), is the world's smallest ocean. It contains the geographic North Pole, which lies under shifting sea ice. Surrounding the ocean are the northern limits of North America and Eurasia. Greenland lies mostly within the Arctic Circle and is permanently iced over.

▲ POLAR BEAR ON SEA ICE
A powerful swimmer, the polar bear hunts seals among the broken sea ice, relying on creamy-yellow fur for camouflage and thick body fat for warmth. It also hunts seals on land, running at speeds up to 34 mph (55 kph), and digs seal pups from their dens in the snow. The bear needs about 4½ lb (2 kg) of fat in its diet per day, and when seals are scarce it eats anything from birds' eggs and fish to seaweed. In the winter, it saves energy by resting in a den. The pregnant female gives birth to two cubs between November and January.

ANTARCTICA

Antarctica is an icebound continent surrounding the South Pole. The ice forms glaciers that shed mighty icebergs into the Southern Ocean. Like the Arctic, Antarctica receives little sunlight: the Sun does not rise at all between late March and September. Even in summer, 85 percent of the Sun's heat is reflected by the ice. So little snow falls each year that the mainland is effectively a cold desert where few animals can survive. But the waters are rich in nutrients, and both the ocean and its remote island groups teem with wildlife.

polar regions

▲ WEATHER STATION
In the early 1900s, explorers battled the intense cold to reach the South Pole. Since the 1950s, Antarctica has been a center for international scientific research. Geologists drill deep into the ice to collect samples laid down thousands of years ago, and use them to measure changes in the world's climate. Fossils show that millions of years ago—before it drifted south and froze—Antarctica was a warm land where trees and reptiles once lived.

◄ ANTARCTICA
Beyond the mainland, the Antarctic includes the Southern Ocean and several islands, such as the Kerguelen, Crozet, South Shetland, and South Orkney groups. The mainland is notched with the Weddell and Ross Seas, and the Antarctic Peninsula threads between them. Sea ice surrounds Antarctica all year, covering 1.6 million sq miles (4 million km²) in summer and 5 times that area in winter.

◄ MAKING AN IGLOO

Humans have lived in the Arctic for thousands of years. They include the Aleut, Inuit, Yupiit, Yakut, and Sami people. The various races range right around the far north, from Alaska, Canada, and Greenland east to Siberia. Traditional families live in an igloo like this or a stone hut. They eat fish, whale, seal, and walrus meat, using other body parts for tools, clothing, and shelters. But today, many communities live modern lifestyles.

Thick skin is flushed pink with blood when on land

Bristles up to 12 in (30 cm) long help the walrus forage on murky sea-beds

WALRUS ►

The walrus is a mammal found in shallow Arctic seas. It gathers in great crowds on sea ice or rocky beaches, where males use their tusks to fight with each other over mates. Awkward on land, the walrus swims powerfully. Thick skin keeps it warm when diving to the sea-bed for clams and mussels, which it finds with stiff bristles on its snout. In spring, the female comes to the beach to give birth to a single calf, which she nurses for about 2 years.

EMPEROR PENGUIN ►

The emperor is the only penguin that breeds solely on the Antarctic mainland. It is an incredible feat. The female lays her egg in May. As she returns to the sea to feed, the male tucks the egg in a pouch under his belly and incubates it through the winter. He huddles with other males for warmth and lives off stored body fat. In July, the fluffy coated chick hatches, and the female finally returns to relieve her starving mate.

Dense, furlike coat of short feathers keeps water out

◄ HUMPBACK WHALE

Humpbacks visit Antarctica during summer to feast on fish and swarms of krill—small, shrimplike crustaceans that feed on plant and animal plankton. Humpback whales are recognizable by having the longest flippers of any animal, with knobbly leading edges. They are extremely vocal, and the male can produce a long, complex series of sounds. Other migrant whales include the blue, pygmy blue, sei, fin, southern right, and minke.

MARINE

The oceans, which make up Earth's largest biome, can be divided into three zones: inshore water, continental margin, and open sea. Oceans are also zoned by depth. The top 660 ft (200 m) is the sunlit zone, where conditions vary greatly. Below it, in the mesopelagic zone, conditions are more stable. The bathypelagic zone, or deep ocean, is a dark and little-studied world of life-forms with extraordinary adaptations.

marine

SQUID ►
The squid feeds on shrimp and small fish in the open seas. It is a mollusc—a group of soft animals without backbones, such as clams and snails. Squid have highly developed nervous systems and superb eyesight. They communicate by rapidly changing skin color.

Two long tentacles with suckered tips for seizing prey and mating

GRAY STARFISH ►
Starfish are not fish at all, but echinoderms, spiny-skinned animals with a central mouth and up to 40 arms. Instead of a single brain they have nerves along the arms, and if an arm is lost a new one soon takes its place. Starfish are predators, feeding on mussels and other shellfish.

Papulae (fleshy lobes) help the starfish to breathe

▲ PARROTFISH
The parrotfish is named after its teeth, which resemble a hard beak. It is vegetarian, nibbling algae from coral surfaces. At night, some species of parrotfish spin a bag of slimy mucus around their bodies. This bag prevents their scent from trailing through the water and stops predators from attacking them in their sleep.

▲ CORAL REEF
Corals are communities of many small individuals called polyps. Each polyp has a soft body in a limestone tube and is permanently attached to other polyps to form rounded, branching or fanlike structures attached to rock. The polyps are nourished by algae living on their surface. The algae need sunlight to survive, so corals are commonly found in shallow, inshore waters.

▲ LOBSTER
The lobster is a crustacean with a hard, jointed shell and four pairs of walking legs. A fifth pair of legs is modified into a pair of powerful claws. The lobster hides in a lair on a sandy or rocky sea-bed, waiting for its prey. Almost anything is on the menu, from small fish to other lobsters as well as plants.

muscular sheath covering organs

Eight true arms with suckers along their length

MYSID SHRIMP
Mysid shrimps are small crustaceans that live in open seas as well as coastal and freshwater habitats. They swarm in vast numbers, filtering tiny particles of food from the water. The females keep their babies in a pouch for several weeks. Mysids are an important prey item for many fish species.

PHYTOPLANKTON
Phytoplankton are tiny, simple organisms, halfway between plant and animal. They survive only in the sunlit zone, where they absorb nutrients from the seawater, and are more common closer to shore than in the open sea. Vast quantities of phytoplankton drift in the currents, forming a living soup on which zooplankton feed.

COPEPOD
Copepods are zooplankton—tiny, swarming animals. Like shrimp, copepods are crustaceans. They have hard shells and many legs. There are over 7,500 copepod species, and their populations number in billions. They feed on phytoplankton and are a source of food for shoaling fishes such as herring.

▲ **CONTINENTAL MARGIN**
When a continent meets an ocean, the gently sloping sea-bed has an average depth of 130 m (430 ft) before falling away steeply farther offshore. This area, known as the continental margin, occupies a small fraction of the total ocean area, but provides some of the richest habitats for sea life, including crustaceans. This is especially true in cooler latitudes, where currents bring nutrients up from nearby deeper water.

▲ **VIPERFISH**
In the dark ocean depths, a hunter has no chance of chasing prey. Prey must be seized at once, or lost. The viperfish has a loose-hinged lower jaw and stretchy stomach for taking in large prey, and its spinelike teeth are angled back to allow no escape. Some species produce light to lure prey near.

▲ **OPEN SEA**
The open sea lacks a rich source of nutrients and is the poorest of ocean habitats. Its most numerous life-forms are plankton—tiny, simple plants and animals, which include fish and crustacean larvae. On the seafloor there is too little light and too much pressure for most life-forms. However, enough organic material sinks down to nourish deep-sea forms of starfish and worms.

OCEANS

The oceans cover more than
70 percent of Earth's surface,
to an average depth of 2.4 miles
(3.8 km). They are home to more than a
quarter of a million known plant and animal species.
Six times as many land species are known to science,
so it is likely that many more ocean species are still to
be discovered when we find the means to explore its depths.
Oceans shape our lives. They provide food, water, medicines,
industrial materials, and energy; they stabilize Earth's
turbulent atmosphere; and they provide transportation
and recreation. Without them there might not be any life.

◄ SUNLIT ZONE
Most fish, turtles, and other large marine
animals are found in the uppermost 660 ft
(200 m), the sunlit or photic zone. The most
numerous life-forms here are the plankton—tiny
animals and plantlike organisms that drift in
the water. They photosynthesize (use sunlight
and nutrients to make energy), and are
the most important source of protein in
marine food webs.

▲ SALT EVAPORATING PONDS
Crystallized salt at the ocean's edge is
formed by evaporation of seawater.
The 3.5% salt content of seawater
comes from minerals containing
chlorine and sodium that are dissolved
from rocks on land and then carried down
rivers to the sea. Undersea volcanoes also pump
minerals into the water. Producing sea salt from
the ocean is a major industry.

oceans

◄ TWILIGHT ZONE
The twilight zone extends to depths of about
3,300 ft (1,000 m). Many midwater animals,
such as herring and squid, rise to the surface at
night to prey on plankton, then sink to deeper
waters by day. The sperm whale, one of the
giants of the twilight zone, illustrates how the
buoyancy of seawater allows ocean creatures to
grow to greater size than land animals, which
have the problem of supporting their weight.

GLOBAL OCEAN CURRENTS

Water continuously moves through all the world's oceans. The Great
Ocean Conveyor is a circulation belt that starts with cold polar water
sinking in the North Atlantic. The cold water flows deep down,
stirring up sea-bed nutrients. It makes the return journey warmed
by tropical Sun. Upwellings of deep water form cold, nutrient-rich
currents off the west coasts of the Americas and Africa. Ocean gyres
are circular flows created by winds on the surface. In the Southern
Ocean, constant west-to-east currents are driven by storm winds.

◄ DEEP-SEA ZONE
The ocean deep is very cold, salty, and pitch-
black. Its few fish tend to be small. Hunters,
such as viperfish, produce chemical light to
lure prey close to their mouths. The sea-bed
crawls with worms, which feed on the drizzle
of organic debris raining down from above.
On deep sea-beds, nutrients bubble up from
volcanic hot springs, supporting a few
organisms that do not depend on oxygen.

THE EXPANSE OF THE OCEAN ►
The world has 5 major oceans: Pacific, Atlantic,
Indian, Arctic, and Southern, in descending order
of size. Each ocean is fringed by seas that cut
into the land margins. The ocean looks flat and
featureless, but immense mountains rise from the
floor. Volcanoes and ridges pour out lava where
oceanic plates meet. Trenches in the ocean
floor reach depths of more than 6.8 miles
(11 km). The oceans contain some
329 million cu miles (1.37 billion km³) of water.

◄ GULF STREAM, FLORIDA
On a satellite map of Florida, the warm waters of the Gulf Stream (orange) show up against the blue-grays of normal sea temperatures. The Gulf Stream is a Sun-warmed current that flows from the Caribbean Sea up the Atlantic coast, stirring up nutrients from the sea-bed and affecting the local climate. Part of the current then heads east to warm Great Britain, while the rest continues as a gyre, or circular current, around the North Atlantic.

USING THE OCEANS

FISHING FOR FOOD
The oceans are our top source of wild protein, with up to 78.6 million tons (80 million tonnes) of seafood caught each year. Key catches include herring, anchovy, cod, hake, and haddock. Some 2 million tons of seaweed are harvested annually to produce foods such as ice cream, as well as medicines. But widespread overfishing means that many fish stocks are now falling.

TRANSPORTATION
It is 10 times cheaper to ship goods by sea than by truck, and 3 times cheaper than by rail. Today, huge cargo vessels ply the oceans laden with cargoes such as crude oil and metal ores. The world's largest oil tanker, *Jahre Viking*, carries more than half a million tons of crude oil. Ship canals, such as the Suez and Panama canals, provide shortcuts between seas and oceans.

ENERGY
The oceans are rich in energy: nearly a third of today's petroleum and natural gas production is from beneath the ocean floor. Depths of up to 8,200 ft (2,500 m) can be reached from ship-mounted drills, although deep drilling is a costly business. Other sources of ocean energy include wave and tidal power, in which the movement of water is converted to electricity through the use of turbines, stationed at sea.

▲ BOAT ON ROUGH SEAS
Storms like these have claimed many lives since humans first went to sea, but they are all part of the water cycle. Water evaporates from the ocean's surface to form storm clouds and unstable air, leading to high winds. Clouds carry the water vapor over land and give us rain. Despite the violence of storms, ocean waters heat up and cool down less rapidly than land, so they help keep the temperature of the atmosphere stable.

Long, narrow, straight wings are ideal for soaring

▲ OCEAN ALBATROSS
The Southern Ocean is home to the wandering albatross *Diomedea exulans*. Its vast wingspan, up to nearly 11 ft (3.5 m), enables it to soar for literally years on end on the constant winds. Landing only to breed on remote cliffs, the albatross may cover 3,700 miles (6,000 km) in less than 2 weeks. It drops to the surface to pluck fish and squid from the water, but also follows fishing boats for scraps.

WAVES AND TSUNAMIS

Waves are a visible sign of energy moving through surface waters. The energy comes from wind on the water, and the more wind, the larger the waves. Ocean waves break as they reach the shore, shaping coastlines through erosion. Wave power offers us a clean source of energy. But waves are also dangerous and can capsize ocean-going vessels during severe storms. The deadliest of all waves are tsunamis: shockwaves triggered by seafloor movements that accompany volcanic eruptions and earthquakes and by large landslides into the sea. Tsunamis can travel at speeds of up to 590 mph (950 kph) and wreak devastation on coastal settlements.

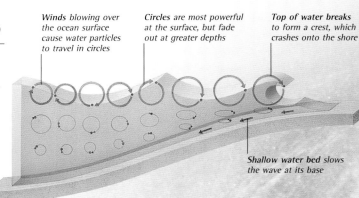

Winds blowing over the ocean surface cause water particles to travel in circles

Circles are most powerful at the surface, but fade out at greater depths

Top of water breaks to form a crest, which crashes onto the shore

Shallow water bed slows the wave at its base

▲ WAVE ACTION
As wave energy advances, it causes water to rotate in circles, or orbits. The uppermost orbits show on the surface as rounded waves, or swell. The wave creates orbits down to a depth of half the wavelength (the distance between two crests). When a wave enters shallows, the deeper orbits drag on the beach and slow the wave's base. Waves become more closely packed. They steepen and form sharp crests, which eventually collapse into breakers.

Face: front wall of wave

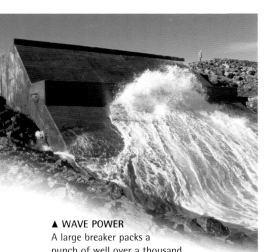

▲ WAVE POWER
A large breaker packs a punch of well over a thousand tons per square centimeter, and in theory the tides and waves offer an endless source of energy. Tidal power plants work by directing the water flow through turbines, which generate electricity. But these are only truly effective where the tidal range (distance in height between high and low tide) is at least 16 ft (5 m), and fewer than 50 sites worldwide offer the right conditions.

LARGE BREAKING WAVE ▶
The biggest ocean waves break on Maui, Hawaii, where some exceed 60 ft (18 m) in height. The Pacific Ocean delivers the biggest breakers because it has the longest fetch—the distance over which wind can blow. The greater the fetch, the greater the wave. Wave energy can travel immense distances; one study tracked swell all the way up the Pacific from Antarctica to the Aleutian Islands, a distance of more than 6,000 miles (10,000 km).

Trough: deepest point between two waves

Reducing water depth slows tsunami

Nearer shore, decreasing depth has a braking effect on the wave

Tsunami grows higher and higher before it finally breaks

	Speed mph (kph)	590 (950)	440 (710)	310 (500)	93 (150)	25 (40)
Sea level (still water level)	Depth ft (m)	23,000 (7,000)	13,000 (4,000)	6,600 (2,000)	3,300 (200)	33 (10)

Submarine earthquake creates shockwave

Fault movement

◀ TSUNAMI
A violent crustal movement may send a wave—a tsunami —across oceans at incredible speeds. At first the wave may be only a yard (meter) or so high and its wavelength extremely long. As the water gets shallower, the bottom of the waves brakes sharply, but the top continues to push forward, until it topples with tremendous force on the shore.

tsunamis

Crest: peak of wave or top of wave height

◄ HILO, HAWAII
Tsunamis cause a lot of the fatalities attributed to earthquakes and volcanoes. A tsunami that swept Hilo, Hawaii, on April 1, 1946, was generated by an earthquake near Unimak, Alaska. Less than five hours later, with no warning, several waves up to 46 ft (14 m) high hit the northeast coast of Hawaii. More than 170 people, including the man in this picture, lost their lives. The Tsunami Warning System (TWS) was set up in response to this disaster.

TSUNAMI RISK AREA

A tsunami can form a broad front that crosses oceans in a few hours. The Hawaiian island chain is most at risk from earthquakes originating along the line of volcanic activity that encircles the Pacific Ocean, known as the "Ring of Fire." After the 1946 tsunami, the US established the Tsunami Warning System (TWS). Based in Honolulu, Hawaii, the TWS generates computer-calculated risk reports. The circular lines on the map are estimates of the time it would take for a wave originating near Valparaiso to reach Honolulu.

Deforested slopes show how high the wave rose

◄ LITUYA BAY, ALASKA
Lituya Bay, Alaska, was the location of the largest wave ever known. On July 9, 1958, an earthquake measuring 7.9 on the Richter Scale struck at the head of Lituya Bay. The tremor caused a landslide into the bay. In one giant mass, 90 million tons of rock fell into the water. The resulting splash wave reached heights of 1,700 ft (520 m) on the surrounding hillsides, snapping trees as though they were matchsticks.

▲ OKUSHIRI, JAPAN
On July 12, 1993, a seafloor earthquake off Hokkaido, Japan, created a tsunami that a few minutes later swept nearby Okushiri Island. It killed 120 people and caused $600 billion worth of damage. Most of the waves reached heights of 50–65 ft (15–20 m), but in one location a valley concentrated the force of the wave, which peaked at a height of more than 100 ft (30 m) and washed away an entire village. Stores of heating fuels caught fire and burned down 340 homes.

EL NINO

Tropical winds and warm ocean currents in the Pacific Ocean usually flow from east to west. But once in every two to seven years the flow reverses, and warm water moves from west to east. Known as El Niño, the reversal brings misery to millions of people by triggering floods, droughts, famine, and disease outbreaks in the Pacific area. Scientists are not sure what causes El Niño, but it coincides with the Southern Oscillation, a reversal in atmospheric pressure in the Pacific. The two effects are so closely linked that they are often simply named the El Niño–Southern Oscillation, or ENSO.

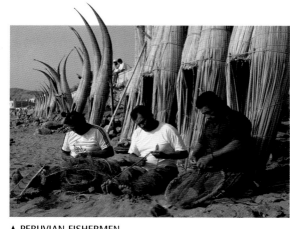

▲ PERUVIAN FISHERMEN
Fishermen in Peru named El Niño, meaning "the child," after the Christ child, because it occurs around Christmas. Their livelihood depends on the cold current that normally flows past the coast. In El Niño years the warm countercurrent is poor in nutrients. The fish starve, or leave the area, and fishing is poor.

▲ FLOODING ON THE CALIFORNIA COAST
Some El Niño years are more severe than others, and weather patterns may be disrupted over a wide area. In 1997–98, one of the worst El Niño seasons on record, fierce storms battered the coast of California. They washed away coastlines and flooded beachfront properties, causing around $550 million worth of damage. That same year, torrential rainfall brought on by disturbed weather patterns also caused floods and landslides across the southern United States.

◄ DROUGHTS IN INDONESIA
An Indonesian farmer picks the last of his parched crop. Low atmospheric pressure over the warm western Pacific Ocean usually brings heavy rainfall to Indonesia, northern Australia, and the Philippines. But during an El Niño year, the eastward flow of warm water takes the rainfall with it, leaving the western Pacific high and dry. In 1997, droughts across Indonesia led to uncontrollable forest fires and crop failures.

El Nino

▲ OCEAN FLOOR

Where continents meet the ocean, the ocean floor deepens to the edge of the continental shelf. The steep continental slope gives way to flat abyssal plains. Great ridges of basalt form at the boundaries of spreading oceanic plates. Where an oceanic plate is subducted (sinks down) beneath a continental plate, a deep trench forms on the ocean floor.

(1) Continental shelf: *shallowly sloping ocean floor at margin of continent*

(2) Continental slope: *steep slope to ocean floor*

(3) Submarine canyon: *formed by erosion*

(4) Continental rise: *gentle slope between abyssal plain and continental slope*

(5) Abyssal plain: *flat ocean floor covered by thin sediment*

(6) Seamount: *submarine volcanic peak*

(7) Guyot: *submarine volcano with an eroded summit*

(8) Midoceanic ridge: *basalt build-up at diverging plate boundary*

(9) Trench: *formed at subduction zone*

(10) Island arc: *volcanic islands formed above subduction zone*

HYDROTHERMAL VENT ▶

Hydrothermal vents are sea-bed hot springs created when seawater contacts hot volcanic rock, then flows back to the sea-bed. The hot springs are also called "black smokers", owing to the colour of suspended minerals in the hot water. Bacteria make sugars for food from carbon dioxide. They are the base of a food chain for more than 300 species, including worms up to 3 m (10 ft) long that live around the vents. Vents were first discovered off the Galapagos Islands in 1977.

"Black smoker" of sulfurous hot water

MID-OCEANIC RIDGE

...AIN

CONTINENTAL SLOPE

▲ DEEPWATER CORAL

Corals usually grow in warm, shallow waters. But scientists using robot submersibles in the North Atlantic and Pacific have filmed cold-water coral reefs at temperatures of 39–54°F (4–12°C) and depths of 9,840 ft (3,000 m). The corals feed by trapping food particles from the water. Most other corals rely on algae living on the reefs to help them build their skeletons. Some governments are writing laws to protect their cold-water reefs from damage by fishing.

e ▸▸

ocean depths

ATMOSPHERE

The atmosphere is an envelope of gases surrounding Earth. It is composed almost entirely of nitrogen, oxygen, and argon, with minute traces of water vapor and other gases. The atmosphere gives us air to breathe and provides water to drink in the form of rain. It protects us from the more harmful energy given out by the Sun, but also traps the Sun's warmth and keeps surface temperatures relatively stable. Without it we would either freeze or burn to a crisp as Earth rotates.

▲ EARTH'S ATMOSPHERE
The view from space reveals the atmosphere as a light haze around the planet. Although it has no upper limit, blending seamlessly into the vacuum of space, it is only in the lowest 62 miles (100 km) that atmospheric density is great enough to screen out harmful solar radiation. The atmosphere makes the Earth unique in the solar system: it is the only planet surrounded by gases that can sustain life.

e ⏭
atmosphere

ATMOSPHERE LAYERS ▶
The atmosphere divides into four unequal layers on the basis of temperature. The outer layer, the thermosphere, is the thickest, extending up to 310 miles (500 km) into space, and is cold at the bottom and very hot at the top. The lowest layer, the troposphere, is only 10 miles (16 km) thick. This layer is warmed by solar heat, and churns with turbulent weather. It contains dust and soil particles, ash from volcanoes and increasingly

▲ DARK CLOUD AND RAIN
The atmosphere is an active element in the water cycle. Water evaporates from the surface of oceans and lakes; the warmer the air, the more water vapor it can hold. The vapor is transported by air currents to the land, where it rises, cools, forms clouds, and falls as rain. The percentage of water vapor in the atmosphere varies: desert air contains almost no vapor at all, whereas the moist air of the humid tropics may hold up to 4% water vapor.

Satellites operate way above the atmosphere in space

75 miles
120 km

68 miles
110 km

Aurora occurs in the thermosphere

62 miles
100 km

56 miles
90 km

50 miles
80 km

43 miles
70 km

37 miles
60 km

31 miles
50 km

25 miles
40 km

Thin layer of ozone absorbs harmful radiation

19 miles
30 km

Jet airliners fly at about 10 km (6 miles) high, in the troposphere

12 miles
20 km

6 miles
10 km

Sea level

140°F
60°C

14°F
-10°C

-112°F
-80°C

Thermosphere
The outermost layer fades into the vacuum of space.

-130°F
-90°C

Meteor burns up due to friction in the atmosphere

-112°F
-80°C

Noctilucent clouds, formed from ice crystals on meteor dust, in the upper mesosphere

Mesosphere
In the mesosphere, temperatures drop as the altitude increases. This layer contains very little water vapour. Its lower limit is called the stratopause or mesopeak, and its upper limit is the mesopause.

-58°F
-50°C

-22°F
-30°C

14°F
-10°C

Stratosphere
The stratosphere is important for its ozone layer at an altitude of about 25 km (16 miles). This layer absorbs ultraviolet radiation from the Sun that would otherwise reach the ground and harm us. Above the ozone layer, radiation causes temperatures in the stratosphere to increase.

-4°F
-20°C

-40°F
-40°C

-76°F
-60°C

Weather is restricted to the troposphere, the lowest level of the atmosphere

-76°F
-60°C

Troposphere
The troposphere is the layer in which we live. The large temperature changes cause mixing of the air, which we experience as weather.

59°F
15°C

Average temperature

▲ SMOG OVER HELSBY, CHESHIRE, UK

Pollution from the factory chimneys creates a smog cloud over this English landscape. Smog contains ozone, which is a form of oxygen whose molecules contain three atoms, unlike the usual two in the oxygen we normally breathe. It occurs mostly in the stratosphere. However, airborne industrial pollutants, such as nitrogen oxides and hydrocarbons, can create ozone at ground level when they react together in the presence of sunlight. Ozone is poisonous, causing lung damage.

▲ OZONE HOLE, 2003

This colored satellite image shows low atmospheric ozone levels over Antarctica. The ozone hole (dark blue) is 10.9 sq miles (28.2 km^2) in size, although it has reduced slightly since 2000 and is predicted to decline over future years. Ozone protects Earth's surface from harmful ultraviolet radiation.

▲ STORMY SEA

Stormy winds are the product of an active atmosphere. Uneven heating of Earth's surface results in an unequal distribution of air pressure. This creates wind, a horizontal movement of air from an area of high pressure to an area of low pressure. The most violent winds—hurricanes—are created when a very large mass of warm, moist air rises. This creates a low-pressure area below, into which air rushes at high speed.

▲ METEOR BARRIER

The atmosphere is not solid, but it acts like a massive, soft wall on meteors and other space rocks. Every day, thousands hurtle through the vacuum of space toward Earth. Friction— the rubbing of the atmosphere on their surface—causes them to burn up before they strike. Only a few are large enough to reach the Earth's surface, and even fewer cause damage. The violent effects of meteor strikes can be seen on the cratered surface of the Moon, which has no atmosphere.

◄ EXTREME COLD
Climate affects people's way of life. Few people choose to live in cold climates, but those who do have come to depend on it. The Inuit people of the Arctic, who use native animals for transportation, food, and clothing, developed such customs from long experience of the local climate. During the winter they hunt seal and walrus from ice on the ocean.

Equator

Inuit wears layers of animal furs to keep out cold

Reindeer are used for food, clothing, and transport

CLIMATE CHANGE

Earth's climates result from interactions of the Sun, the atmosphere, Earth, and the watery part of the Earth's surface—especially the oceans. We use the word climate to describe how we expect the weather to behave in any place. Climates vary from one region to the next because of differences in sunlight, temperature, rainfall, winds, ocean currents, and landshapes. Climate also changes on a global scale. In the past, Earth has been both warmer and colder than today. Scientists suspect that we may now be helping to warm the world's climate by adding carbon dioxide to the atmosphere through burning coal, oil, and natural gas.

PACIC OCEAN

ARCTIC OCEAN

USA

Laurentide Ice Sheet

North Pole

Siberian Ice Sheet

ATLANTIC OCEAN

KEY

☐ Ice Sheet
▷ Direction of ice flow
☐ Sea ice
☐ Land created by low sea level

Camel allows its body temperature to rise by day, then loses excess heat at night

Cover-up clothing defends against the Sun's fierce heat and sandstorms

Hollow drill pipe for extracting ice core

◄ EXTREME HEAT
Here, a Tuareg camel herder tends his camels in the North African desert. The German scientist Wladimir Köppen invented a system of classifying Earth's many different climates. He put them into five broad groups according to temperature and rainfall. Köppen's system describes the desert climate as one where the rate of rainfall cannot catch up with the rate of evaporation: there is always a lack of water. Like the Inuit in the Arctic, the Tuareg people of North Africa—and the camel—have adapted to survive in an extreme climate.

▲ SATELLITE MAP OF THE WORLD'S AVERAGE TEMPERATURE
Temperature, along with rainfall, is the key factor affecting climate. This map shows the world's average temperature in January, ranging from -29°F (-34°C), shown in mauve, to 61–93°F (16–34°C), shown in pink and red, and 97–104°F (36–40°C), shown in dark red and black (as in Australia). Despite this wide variance, today's global climate is more moderate than at many earlier periods in Earth's history. One hundred million years ago, the world may have been more than 11°F (6°C) warmer than today.

climate

DRILLING FOR DEEP-SEA SEDIMENT CORE ▲
Scientists retrieve a core of sediment from the ocean floor. Sea-bed samples are a useful record of Earth's climate history. For example, they contain layers of microscopic fossils that are sensitive to sea temperatures, and are therefore good indicators of past climate change. Rock fragments carried out to sea and dumped by icebergs reveal where and when glaciers were active on land.

◄ EXTENT OF THE LAST GLACIATION
During the last Ice Age, which ended 10,000–15,000 years ago, ice covered 30% of the land. The North Polar ice cap grew to cover 7.3 million sq miles (19 million km²) of North America, Siberia, and Europe. (The southern ice cap was restricted to the land mass of Antarctica, as today.) Sea levels fell, having supplied the water vapor that created the snow and ice. The lowering sea levels exposed new areas of land on the margins of continents. These included a land bridge between North America and Siberia.

Clouds of volcanic ash erupting from Mount St. Helens in 1980

ice sample taken from depths up to 11,800 ft (3,600 m)

◄ GEOLOGISTS STUDYING ICE CORE
Glaciations occur when low global temperatures create greater ice cover. Geologists study ice core samples to learn when, and for how long, glaciations took place. For example, the last Ice Age began 3 million years ago and consisted of 20 glaciations spaced about 100,000 years apart. Ancient ice reveals other clues about climate. Each layer preserves carbon dioxide and methane gas, dust, volcanic ash, and pollen, forming a record of the atmosphere at that time. The oldest known glaciation occurred about 2.3 billion years ago.

VOLCANIC ASH FROM MOUNT ST. HELENS ▲
Erupting volcanoes send millions of tons of ash and gas, including sulfur dioxide, into the atmosphere. The sulfur dioxide gas mixes with water vapor to make clouds of very tiny droplets of sulfuric acid. These scatter sunlight back into space, causing Earth's surface to cool. Huge eruptions, like that of Tambora in Indonesia in 1815, can cool global temperatures for more than a year.

Deep, dark cumulonimbus clouds form as cold air forces moist warm air upward

Cold front forms as cold air pushes against warm air

◄ ADVANCING COLD FRONT OVER FLORIDA
An aerial view shows a cold, high-pressure air mass (lower right) moving into a warm, low-pressure air mass (upper left). When a cold mass invades a warm mass, the boundary is called a cold front. Clouds of different types form along the front, the line where they meet. A deep bank of cumulonimbus clouds shows where dense cold air is forcing lighter warm air to rise steeply and shed water vapor.

Warm air glides up over cold air

◄ WARM FRONT
When a warm air mass advances after a retreating cold air mass, the boundary between them is termed a warm front. The cold air sinks to the ground and the warm air moves overhead, so the front becomes a shallow slope. The warm air cools as it mounts the slope, creating a range of cloud forms. The lowest clouds release moderate rainfall.

Rain falls at low altitudes along front

Warm front weather map symbol

WEATHER

Our everyday weather is controlled by the local behavior of the atmosphere. Warm spells, overcast days, and sudden cold showers all result from the movement of air masses. Large air masses typically have a uniform temperature and air pressure, so they may bring several days of stable weather while passing overhead. But when two different air masses collide, a change in weather occurs along the boundary, or front, between them. The factors that affect air pressure and movement range from the height of local mountain ranges to global wind and ocean currents.

COLD FRONT ►
When a cold air mass advances rapidly into a warm mass, the front is steeply sloped, and the warm air is forced to rise quickly. If the rising air is moist, water condenses from it to form towering cumulonimbus clouds. The energy circulating in the clouds produces thunderstorms and heavy, but brief, rainfall.

Cold air pushes warm air upward

Rising warm air produces thunderclouds and heavy rain

Cold front weather map symbol

Occluded front weather map symbol

Cold air catches up with warm air

Rising warm air sheds heavy rain

◄ OCCLUDED FRONT
Occluded means "trapped," and this occurs when a warm front advances into cool air but is then overtaken by a cold front. The cold front wheels around behind and pushes up the warm air mass, which sheds heavy rainfall. The new, occluded front is formed between the three air masses.

GLOBAL MOVEMENT OF WINDS

POLAR EASTERLIES
WESTERLIES
NE TRADES
NE TRADES
SW MONSOON
NE TRADES
DOLDRUMS
DOLDRUMS
DOLDRUMS
SE TRADES
SE TRADES
SE TRADES
WESTERLIES
WESTERLIES
POLAR EASTERLIES

Winds blowing toward the equator are deflected west by the Earth's rotation. These winds, known as the trades or trade winds, die down near the equator to create a still belt known as the doldrums. In the temperate zones, the prevailing winds are westerlies (blowing from the west), which are also governed by the Earth's rotation. Cold, dry, easterly winds blow from the constant high-pressure zones over the North and South poles. On large landmasses, the monsoon—a seasonal change in land and sea temperatures—leads to wet onshore winds in summer and dry offshore winds in winter.

WIND ►
Wind is the movement of air from colder, high-pressure zones to warmer, low-pressure zones. It reacts rapidly to a change in conditions, as can be seen on many coastlines. At night, the land cools more rapidly than the sea, so winds blow offshore from the cool to the warm zone. By day, the pressures are reversed. The land warms up more rapidly than the sea, creating low pressure and attracting onshore winds.

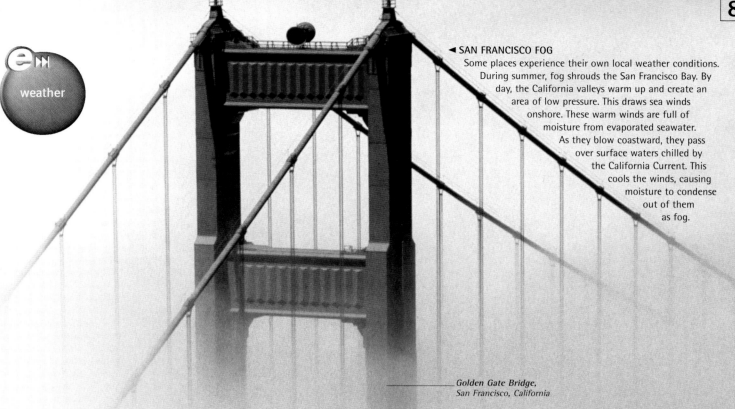

e ▸▸
weather

◂ SAN FRANCISCO FOG
Some places experience their own local weather conditions. During summer, fog shrouds the San Francisco Bay. By day, the California valleys warm up and create an area of low pressure. This draws sea winds onshore. These warm winds are full of moisture from evaporated seawater. As they blow coastward, they pass over surface waters chilled by the California Current. This cools the winds, causing moisture to condense out of them as fog.

Golden Gate Bridge,
San Francisco, California

HOW MOUNTAINS AFFECT WEATHER

ALPS
Mountains strongly affect local weather conditions. High-pressure systems over mountains send cold winds rushing down the slopes into the valleys below. In southern France, the Mistral—a dry, icy wind from the Alps—funnels down the Rhône valley at high speed, and is a key weather-maker in France's Provence region.

FOREST FIRES
The mountains of southern California force winds to speed up as they pass overhead or are funneled through narrow passes. By the time the winds descend the other side, they are drained of all moisture. Hot and dry, these Santa Ana winds parch the valley vegetation and seriously increase the risk of forest fires.

DESERT SNOW ▴
Weather is full of surprises, and can change dramatically from day to day. The Mojave desert in the southwest of North America bakes during the summer and receives less than 6 in (150 mm) of annual precipitation, but it is not a hot desert. It lies at high altitudes in a temperate zone. Temperatures may plummet to 9°F (–13°C) in winter, and the vegetation, including the Joshua Tree yucca, has to be prepared for sudden snowfalls.

◂ SATELLITE WEATHER IMAGING
A satellite image shows atmospheric conditions over the US. Spacecraft and radar are just two of the instruments used by meteorologists to analyze and forecast the weather. This service is vital: an estimated 80% of US national emergencies are linked to extreme weather conditions. As well as national forecasts, predictions are made for large cities, which give out so much heat and pollution that they create their own conditions.

PRECIPITATION

Precipitation is the name given to water and ice that collect on the Earth's surface from the atmosphere. It is a feature of water's remarkable ability to transform rapidly between solid (ice), liquid (rain and dew), or gas (water vapor) within a narrow temperature range. Many parts of the world enjoy moderate rainfall, but some regions are permanently parched while others suffer disastrous floods. Where rain and snow fall, and for how long, depends a lot on location, season, and the shape of the land.

◄ RAIN

Rain is caused by the movement of air masses. When moist, warm air rises it expands, loses energy, and cools. Cool air can hold less moisture than warm air. So water condenses out of it in clouds of countless tiny droplets. Dust or ice crystals in the clouds collect water droplets and grow into raindrops. Many factors can make warm air create rain clouds. These include frontal wedging, convergence, and mountain lifting, which are illustrated below.

RAIN CLOUD FORMATION

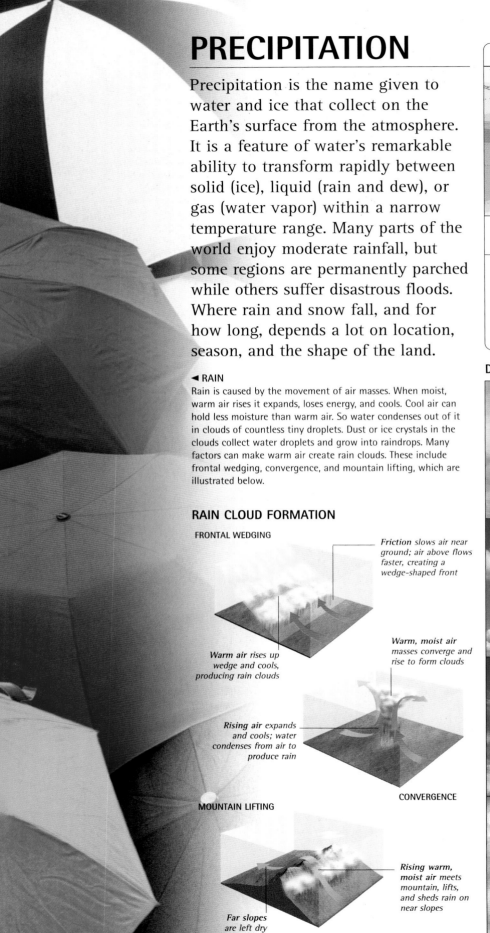

FRONTAL WEDGING

Friction slows air near ground; air above flows faster, creating a wedge-shaped front

Warm air rises up wedge and cools, producing rain clouds

Warm, moist air masses converge and rise to form clouds

Rising air expands and cools; water condenses from air to produce rain

CONVERGENCE

MOUNTAIN LIFTING

Rising warm, moist air meets mountain, lifts, and sheds rain on near slopes

Far slopes are left dry

WORLD PRECIPITATION

KEY

▓ 120 – 160 in	▒ 40 – 80 in	□ 10 – 20 in
▓ 80 – 120 in	▒ 20 – 40 in	□ 0 – 10 in

Tropical regions receive high rainfall because the ocean warmth leads to high evaporation, which increases the amount of moisture in the air. Polar regions are dry because cold air holds so little moisture. The large landmass of Asia creates low pressure during summer, which draws moist winds in from the ocean. High pressure in winter drives dry winds toward the ocean. This seasonal wind change is called the monsoon. Mountain ranges affect rainfall, too, by driving warm air upward, which cools it, condenses water vapor, and creates rain.

DIFFERENT CLOUD TYPES

STRATUS
This term comes from a word meaning "layer" and describes clouds that form a more-or-less even layer. Like other cloud terms it can be used in combination. Nimbostratus is a gray layer of rain clouds at low altitude. Altostratus is a thinner, whiter layer at middle altitudes. Cirrostratus describes a thin, bright, high-altitude haze.

CUMULUS
Cumulus resembles a mass of rounded domes. Often the base is flat. These puffy clouds form at high altitude (cirrocumulus), mid-altitude (altocumulus), and low altitude (cumulus). These fluffy, "cotton ball" clouds are characteristic of fair weather, but deep masses of cumulus with thick, dark bases are storm clouds and a sign of approaching rain.

CIRRUS
Cirrus clouds are very high, thin, and wispy, because of the low water vapor content at high altitude. They consist of ice crystals and are a bright, reflective white. Some, known as mare's tails, look like fine strands of hair. Cirrus clouds do not themselves produce rain, but may be the first sign of an approaching warm front, promising rain later.

CUMULONIMBUS
Uprushing warm air masses can create towering clouds known as cumulonimbus up to 11 miles (18 km) deep. As the warm air rises and cools, it forms clouds and releases energy, and if it is still warmer than the surrounding air, it keeps moving upward. Cumulonimbus clouds are a source of thunderstorms, and their upper levels may contain snow or hail.

▲ SNOW

Snowflakes grow in clouds of supercooled vapor – water droplets that remain liquid way below their normal freezing point. Supercooled vapor rapidly freezes onto any available surface, so when ice crystals are present it clings to them, making them larger. As the flakes grow, gravity makes them fall. Snow reaches the ground only if air temperatures lower down remain cold. Snowflakes are usually clumps of several ice crystals.

SNOW CRYSTAL

▼ THUNDER AND LIGHTNING

Thunderstorms are created by unstable air movements within cumulonimbus clouds. Rain and hail move so vigorously that they gather an electrical charge. Positive charges cluster high in the cloud, while negative charges cluster lower down. When the electrical resistance breaks down, lightning flashes between the two within the cloud and sometimes between the cloud and the ground. The thunder we hear is the sound of nearby air being heated to temperatures of 36,000°F (20,000°C)—three times hotter than the surface of the Sun. This compresses the surrounding air, which produces a shockwave.

Positively charged hail and rain gather in high cloud

New layer of ice freezes around the hailstone

Raindrop freezes into hailstone

Hailstone is too heavy to be held in the cloud and falls to the ground

Updraugh carries raindrop up

Raindrop

Hailstone falls

Negatively charged hail and rain in low cloud mass

▲ HOW HAIL FORMS

Like snow, a hailstone starts life as a raindrop in a very cold cloud. But hail forms only in huge clouds containing powerful updraughts of wind. The hailstone first falls a little, collecting droplets of supercooled water vapor. Then updraughts carry the hailstone up again and more water vapor freezes onto it. This process continues until the hailstone falls. Most hailstones are pea-sized, but some are as big as oranges.

HUGE HAILSTONES

Negative electrical charge from cloud leaps to positive ground through a lightning bolt

precipitation

▲ ATACAMA IN CHILE

One of the world's driest places is the Atacama desert in Chile. The town of Iquique receives heavy rain less than five times a century. The dry conditions are due partly to the Andes mountains.

▲ CHERRAPUNJI, INDIA

Some of the world's highest rainfall is in the foothills of the Himalayas and nearby plateaus in northern India. During the summer monsoon (wind change), wet winds blow north from the Indian Ocean.

Ground is positively charged and attracts negative charge

WEATHER FORECASTING

A timely warning of bad weather can save lives and property. Meteorology—the study of weather—is based on scientific observation of the atmosphere. Meteorologists collect readings of wind, temperature, pressure, and other conditions from weather stations on land and sea all over the world. The figures are analysed by powerful computers and shared between nations to produce the weather maps and forecasts we see on television. With modern technology, forecasters can predict weather several days into the future.

TYPHOON TOM

TYPHOON VIOLET

High pressure brings clear skies and no precipitation

Thick cloud in the depression bringing rain and snow

Japan

▲ NSCAT IMAGE SHOWING TYPHOON ACTIVITY AROUND JAPAN
Radar signals from satellites and aircraft tell meteorologists about ocean wind conditions. This map of the Pacific shows fast winds in orange and slow winds in blue. The swirls near Japan are hurricanes, or typhoons. Typhoon Violet, to the south, blew into Tokyo on September 22, 1993, killing 3 people. The larger typhoon, Tom, headed east and blew out safely. The image was created by a scatterometer, which sends radar signals from a satellite to the sea surface and "reads" the echoes that return. This image was gathered by a NASA Scatterometer (NSCAT) instrument on an weather satellite.

weather

Air pressure in hectopascals (millibars)

High atmospheric pressure center

Cloud cover indicating overcast

Black spot indicates rain

◄ SATELLITE IMAGE AND CORRESPONDING WEATHER MAP
The satellite photograph and chart shows a developing low-pressure system, or depression, over Japan. The image, along with readings from many weather stations, helped meteorologists compose the weather map below it. Strong winds sweep counterclockwise around the low pressure center, bringing warm and cold fronts with them. The symbols plotted on the map show weather fronts, surface conditions (such as rain), wind speed and direction, and air pressure.

Close spacing of isobars indicates strong winds associated with low-pressure systems

High pressure centres bring light winds and settled dry weather

HIGH PRESSURE

HIGH PRESSURE

Occluded front usually associated with low-pressure system

Advancing cold front

Warm front

"Arrow" indicates direction of wind; "feathers" indicate its strength

HIGH PRESSURE

LOW PRESSURE

HIGH PRESSURE

◄ GOES SATELLITE
The US geostationary operational environmental satellite (GOES) remains in the same location above Earth. It measures atmospheric temperature, moisture, and winds, and also collects readings transmitted from weather buoys in the oceans. All the data is beamed down to Earth for analysis by the National Weather Service.

AIR PRESSURE MAP ►
Air pressure is the weight of the atmosphere over a unit area of Earth's surface. Changes of weather are usually accompanied by changes in air pressure so isobaric maps are needed for accurate weather forecasting. Isobars, the lines on a pressure map, connect points of equal pressure. The low-pressure center shown here over the English Channel indicates high winds and heavy rain.

Long nose probe samples air outside the aircraft's influence

Trade winds (red) to north and south of equator

Anemometer measures wind speed and direction

Solar panel provides power outside winter months

▲ SNOOPY THE WEATHER PLANE

Weather aircraft serve an important role in sampling the atmosphere. *Snoopy*, a heavily modified Hercules transport plane, was used from 1972 to 2001 to conduct atmospheric research around the world. Its scientific instruments took a wide range of readings including atmospheric radiation, ozone, nitrogen content, and cloud density. The aircraft also released radio-sondes, probes that fell by parachute and sampled a vertical cross-section of the atmosphere.

◄ AUTOMATIC WEATHER STATION

Unmanned weather stations are especially useful in remote areas of the world. This is one of several automatic weather stations that record surface conditions on Antarctica. Some are positioned on icebergs in the ocean. Automatic weather stations measure temperature, pressure, humidity, and wind speed and direction. At regular intervals every day, they transmit readings via satellite to monitoring centers all over the world.

WEATHER BALLOON LAUNCH ►

An atmosphere researcher launches the daily weather balloon at his Antarctic base. The helium balloon carries a radiosonde, a sensor that takes a series of atmospheric readings as it rises. At an altitude of about 16 miles (25 km), low air pressure causes the balloon to burst, and the instrument returns to the ground by parachute. Balloon radiosondes are useful for measuring ozone in the upper atmosphere, enabling environmental change to be monitored.

Anemometer

▲ WEATHER BUOY

This is one of a network of moored weather buoys that operate in US waters. The buoys record wind and sea conditions in order to improve the accuracy of shipping forecasts and avert disasters such as coastal floods. Several countries run weather buoy networks. Along with data from satellites and weather stations, the buoy readings are transmitted over the Global Telecommunications System, an international network that shares weather data.

◄ WEATHER PLOTTING

In Bracknell, the headquarters of the UK Meteorological Office, computers combine data from weather recording stations in the UK. Surface readings are sent in by about 200 land stations and 600 ships and rigs, which form part of a 7,000-strong international fleet. Balloons and satellites provide upper-air readings, and a network of weather radars reports on rainfall. The computers provide nowcasting (short-term forecasts), as well as long-term forecasts.

TORNADOES

Tornadoes, also known as twisters, are the most violent of all winds, reaching speeds of up to 300 mph (480 kph). They take the form of a slender, whirling column, created when warm air is sucked into the zone of low air pressure beneath a thundercloud. A tornado releases immense energy as it tracks across the land, and can splinter houses or hurl trucks through the air. Though tornadoes strike many parts of the world, they are a particular menace on the North American prairies, where they kill around 60 people every year.

GLOBAL TORNADO ACTIVITY

Tornado activity (marked in orange on this map) tends to occur in temperate regions, and in the central US in particular, where the region from North Dakota south to Texas is known as "Tornado Alley." Tornadoes are common there in spring, when cold polar air meets warm, moist air from the Gulf of Mexico. The mixing air masses create cyclones, low-pressure zones where warm air rises in spirals. Throughout the northern hemisphere, tornadoes rotate counter-clockwise, corresponding to the spin of cyclones. In the southern hemisphere, cyclones spin clockwise, and so do most tornadoes.

FORMATION OF A TORNADO

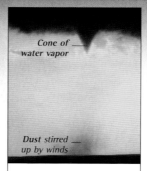

Cone of water vapor

Dust stirred up by winds

1. FIRST SIGNS
It is widely thought that tornadoes touch down from a cloud to the ground. They do not. A mesocyclone (wide column of revolving air) already connects the cloud base and ground surface. Here, flying dust and a cone of cloud vapor are telltale signs of a mesocyclone.

Cooling air creates more water vapor

Faster winds stir more dust

2. COLUMN FORMS
The tornado is underway. As warm, moist air rushes into the base of the column and spirals upward, it expands rapidly and cools. This causes it to release water vapor in the form of a cloud. It is the cloud, along with dust sucked up from below, that makes the column visible.

3. PEAK POWER
A tornado normally lasts a few minutes, but the strongest ones can last an hour or more. It decays when the supply of warm, moist air from the base runs out, or when draughts of cool, dry air sink from the cloud. The tornado often tightens into a slender rope of wind before dying away.

Funnel of visible cloud (water vapor) descends into column

Large air masses revolve, creating wide column of rotating air

Rotating air increases speed as column narrows

Rising warm air creates low pressure at ground level

Base of tornado causes localized destruction

WARM AIR RUSHES IN

▲ ANATOMY OF A TORNADO
Warm, moist air rushes up into a big thundercloud known as a supercell, and rubs against cold air higher up. The two air masses turn around each other and create a mesocyclone—a wide column of revolving air. The mesocyclone spins faster as it sucks in more warm air. In about 50% of cases, the mesocyclone generates a really fast, destructive column of air—a tornado.

▲ ROPE TORNADO
A rope tornado is a long, slender wind column. It is often the mark of a tornado nearing the end of its life, though some tornadoes remain ropelike from start to finish. While rope tornadoes may roam erratically, they always remain attached to the storm cloud. They are no less destructive than wide tornados; in fact, as a column tightens, its wind speed increases, just as ice-skaters speed up as they draw up into a pirouette.

◄ TORNADO DAMAGE, US, 1998
Tornadoes are the biggest threat to life and property in parts of the US, destroying everything in their path. In the Midwest, and particularly over the Mississippi valley, conditions are often right for tornadoes to develop. An extreme tornado, with winds over 300 mph (450 kph), can pick objects up and hurl them like bullets, strip a person's clothes off, or tear the roofs off houses, as shown here.

TRI-STATE TORNADO, 1925 ►
The longest-lasting and most destructive tornado in recorded history struck the US states of Missouri, Illinois, and Indiana on March 18, 1925. The so-called Tri-State Tornado raced northeastward for 219 miles (352 km) at speeds of up to 73 mph (118 kph), leaving a trail of devastation. It wiped out several villages, killed 695 people, and injured more than 2,000.

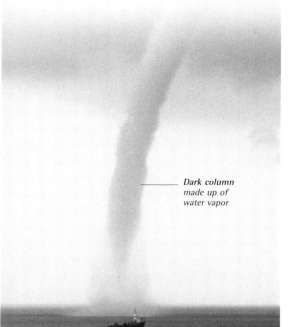

Dark column made up of water vapor

Dish for Doppler radar tracking

▲ WATERSPOUT
A waterspout is simply another name for a tornado over water. Though it looks like a solid column of water, it is mostly water vapor, which condenses out of rising warm air. Waterspouts are common over tropical and subtropical seas, where there is a ready supply of warm, moist air. They have the peculiar habit of picking up fish and frogs and dropping them over land.

tornadoes

▲ TRUCK-MOUNTED DOPPLER RADAR DISH
Radar helps experts give tornado warnings, and a form of radar known as Doppler has been in use since 1973. This detects mesocyclones, and can also track the direction of moving masses of rain and hail in big thunderclouds. In the United States, a network of fixed Doppler radar sites across the country keeps constant watch. This truck-mounted Doppler radar is used by "stormchasers," who follow tornadoes to study them at close quarters.

THE FUJITA SCALE ►
The Fujita Scale grades tornadoes by the damage they cause. Sixty-six percent of the tornadoes reported annually in the United States are listed F0 and F1. The 2% that make up F4 and F5 account for more than two-thirds of fatalities.

THE FUJITA SCALE

F0	F1	F2	F3	F4	F5
Light damage: less than 73 mph (118 kph); some broken branches and chimneys	Moderate damage: 73–112 mph (118–180 kph); roofs peeled back, cars blown about	Considerable damage: 113–157 mph (182–253 kph); roofs torn off frame houses	Severe damage: 158–206 mph (254–332 kph); trains overturned, trees uprooted	Devastating damage: 207–260 mph (333–419 kph); well-built houses leveled	Incredible damage: 261–318 mph (420–512 kph); car-sized missiles fly through air

The eye of the storm, a calm area up to 31 miles (50 km) across

Whirling winds around the eye may reach speeds of up to 224 mph (360 kph)

HURRICANES

Hurricanes are the world's most destructive weather systems. They begin when thunderstorms mass together around a central area of low pressure. Also known as tropical cyclones, hurricanes form over tropical oceans, where warm waters create the necessary conditions. Once hurricanes have taken shape, they may travel thousands of miles, leaving a trail of devastation and breaking up only on reaching cold water or land. Scientists monitor hurricanes constantly in order to warn people living in high-risk zones, such as the Caribbean or the Bay of Bengal.

hurricanes

▲ PROGRESS OF HURRICANE

This sequence of images shows Hurricane Andrew approaching Florida (from right to left) on August 24, 1992. The telltale spiral shape of a hurricane is created by cloud and rain bands sucked in toward the eye by spiraling winds. Meteorologists give personal names to hurricanes to encourage the public to listen to warning messages. At first, tropical cyclones were named after unpopular Australian politicians; today, men, women, animals, and trees all lend their names to storms.

Dry air descends into low-pressure eye of storm

High level winds spiral outward

◄ HURRICANE CROSS-SECTION

The heart of a hurricane is the eye, a column of calm air. Around it is the eyewall: a funnel of storm winds rotating at speeds of 75 mph (120 kph) or more. The eyewall carries warm, moist air upward. This updraught creates low pressure at ground level, drawing in more warm air. The rising air cools and sheds torrential rain, then is hurled out over the storm clouds. Farther out, thunderstorms are fed by inrushing warm air to form towering walls of wind, clouds, and rain.

Fastest winds spiral around the eyewall

Sea surface rises in the low-pressure eye area

Spiraling bands of wind and rain

► BEAUFORT SCALE

The Beaufort Scale was devised in 1805 as a way of measuring wind speed at sea. Its 13 divisions range from calm conditions to hurricane force. In 1955, they were extended to 18 by the Saffir-Simpson Hurricane Scale, used to describe extremely violent storms.

①	②	③	④	⑤
Light air: Average wind speed 2 mph (3 kph). Chimney smoke drifts gently.	**Light breeze**: Wind speed 5 mph (9 kph). Leaves rustle. Wind felt on your face.	**Gentle breeze**: Wind speed 10 mph (15 kph). Leaves and twigs on trees move. Flags flutter.	**Moderate wind**: Wind speed 15 mph (25 kph). Small branches move. Paper blows around.	**Fresh wind**: Wind s 22 mph (35 kph). S trees start to sway.

Spiral bands of cloud surround the eye

GLOBAL HURRICANE ACTIVITY

As their name indicates, tropical cyclones form only in tropical oceans. They are never less than five degrees north or south of the equator, on account of the Coriolis effect. This is when wind and ocean currents approaching the equator are pushed aside by Earth's rotational force. The Coriolis effect puts the first spin on a developing cyclone. To create the tremendous energy required to fuel a cyclone, the water temperature must be warm—at least 80°F (26.5°C) to a depth of 164 ft (50 m) or more. The heat and moisture not only start the cyclone, but also feed it. This explains why cyclones run out of energy when they cross cold ocean waters.

▼ AFTERMATH OF ANDREW

Boats lie heaped like toys after Hurricane Andrew's passage over Florida in 1992. Andrew was a relatively small hurricane: Hurricane Gilbert (1988) was five times the size. However, Andrew's winds were particularly violent, with gusts of up to 163 mph (262 kph). The hurricane destroyed more than 80,000 homes and caused $26.5 billion worth of damage before it ran into the coast of Louisiana and broke up.

HURRICANE HUNTERS

In the United States, pilots of the 53rd Weather Reconnaissance Squadron search for tropical cyclones forming in the Atlantic, Caribbean Sea, Gulf of Mexico, and the eastern Pacific. They fly specially modified aircraft, carrying monitoring equipment, right into the eye of the storm. Telltale signs are storm clouds massing together around low-pressure areas. Sensors on parachutes are dropped into the storm to record temperature, wind speed, air pressure, and humidity. The readings are sent to the National Hurricane Center in Miami for analysis, and then distributed to meteorological centers around the world.

TREES UPROOTED BY STORM, KENT, UK ►

The "Great Storm" that struck southern England on October 15–16, 1987, was the worst recorded since 1703. The 62-mph (100-kph) winds were well below hurricane force, but uprooted more than 15 million trees. They were in part caused by a true hurricane. Hurricane Floyd had hit the Caribbean a few days earlier and sent jet-stream winds thousands of miles east across the Atlantic toward Great Britain. These cold winds ran into warm, moist winds from the south, causing the storm.

⑦	⑧	⑨	⑩	⑪	⑫
g wind: Wind h (45 kph). Hard trol umbrella. branches move.	**Near gale:** Wind speed 35 mph (56 kph). Whole trees sway.	**Gale:** Wind speed 42 mph (68 kph). Difficult to walk. Twigs broken off trees.	**Severe gale:** Wind speed 50 mph (81 kph). Roof tiles and chimney tops blown off.	**Storm:** Wind speed 58 mph (94 kph). Houses damaged. Trees blown down.	**Severe storm:** Wind speed 68 mph (110 kph). Serious damage.

Hurricane: Wind speed more than 73 mph (118 kph). Widespread damage.

TIMELINE OF EARTH DISCOVERIES

discoveries

c.585BC According to the writers of his day, Thales of Miletus (in modern-day Turkey) correctly predicts a solar eclipse.

c.450BC Greek statesman Empedocles puts forward theory that everything is made entirely of four elements—earth, air, fire, and water—mixed in different proportions.

c.280BC Greek astronomer Aristarchus is the first to estimate the distance between the Earth and the Sun. He is also the first to suggest that the planet rotates on its axis and revolves around the Sun, though few people believe him.

c.240BC Eratosthenes of Cyrene studies the angles of sunlight falling on two towns in Egypt, and from them he measures the circumference of Earth as 25,700 miles (41,143 km). He is accurate to within 800 miles (1,000 km).

AD23 Greek geographer and historian Strabo publishes his *Geographical Sketches*. In them he notes that earthquakes and volcanoes cause lands to rise and sink; he proposes cold, temperate, and tropical climate zones; and he suggests Earth is so big there might be continents still to discover.

AD79 Roman Pliny the Younger writes the first account of a volcanic eruption, describing Mount Vesuvius.

c.130 Chinese scientist Chang Heng designs the first seismograph. His "earthquake weathercock" uses finely balanced metal balls that fall when the ground shakes.

c.140 Greek astronomer and mathematician Ptolemy claims the Earth is at the center of the Universe, and that the Sun and planets revolve around it.

c.975 Muslim scholars in Basra (Iraq) publish *The Aim of the Sage*, an encyclopedia that describes rock layers.

1086 Chinese astronomer and engineer Shen Kua describes rock erosion, sedimentation, and uplift and explains the origins of fossils.

c.1100 Chinese invent the magnetic compass. It uses a pivoting magnetized needle to point to Earth's poles.

1492 Genoese merchant Christopher Columbus is sponsored by Spain to find a western route to China. But his maps (based on Ancient Greek and Biblical geography) are wrong. He lands in the Caribbean instead (believing it to be Japan), and is credited with discovering America.

c.1500 Italian artist and scientist Leonardo da Vinci suggests that fossil shells in hillside rocks are remains of animals that once lived in the sea.

1519–21 Portuguese navigator Ferdinand Magellan sets out to be the first to sail around the world. He is killed in the Philippines, but his surviving sailors complete the circumnavigation.

c.1540 German scientist Georgius Agricola publishes a scientific classification of minerals (then known as fossils).

1543 Polish astronomer Nicolaus Copernicus publishes his theory that Earth rotates on its axis daily and revolves annually around the Sun.

1600 English scientist William Gilbert publishes his experiments which showed that the Earth is a giant magnet, whose north and south poles roughly coincide with its geographic poles.

1609 Italian astronomer Galileo Galilei uses a telescope to offer the first scientific proof for Copernicus's theory. Using his telescope, Galileo found that Venus went through phases, just like our Moon, and that these phases could only be explained by Venus going around the Sun and not the Earth.

1620 English thinker Francis Bacon notices that the coasts of Africa and South America fit like pieces of a jigsaw.

1644 Italian physicist Evangelista Torricelli invents the mercury barometer, an instrument that measures atmospheric pressure.

1650 English Archbishop James Ussher adds up the ages of characters in the Bible to calculate the birth of the Universe in 4004 BC. His view is widely accepted until the 19th century.

1655 Ferdinand II, grand duke of Tuscany and a pupil of Galileo, invents the condensation hygrometer (which measures humidity) and the thermometer (which measures temperature).

1669 Danish geologist Nicolaus Steno describes crystal formation in quartz. He recognizes that some rocks are formed from sediment, and that the Earth's history can be studied by looking at rock layers.

1679 English astronomer Edmund Halley recognizes that the Sun's warmth creates atmospheric movement, and links air pressure with altitude. He predicts the return of Halley's comet in 1705.

1687 English scientist Isaac Newton publishes *Mathematical Principles of Natural Philosophy* (known as the *Principia*), which sets out to explain the basic laws that govern motion, gravity, and the Universe.

1735 English physicist George Hadley explains how Earth's rotation affects trade winds. His name is given to Hadley cells, which are an element of global air circulation patterns.

1795 Scottish geologist James Hutton challenges the popular Bible-based belief that the Earth is only 6,000 years old. He claims that the processes now shaping Earth's crust (such as sedimentation and erosion) have been doing so for much longer.

1804 French zoologist Georges Cuvier, studies ancient fossils and suggests they are "thousands of centuries" old. He believes that long-extinct animals were killed off by natural catastrophes, such as floods.

1806 English Admiral Francis Beaufort devises a scale of wind speed for sailors at sea. It was later modified for land use by substituting features such as cars and trees.

1815 English engineer William Smith publishes the first geologic map. He shows that, depending on where they are found in rock layers, fossils prove whether one layer is older than another.

1822 English amateur paleontologist Mary Anne Mantell discovers the first fossils (large teeth) of a giant creature, later identified as a dinosaur by English scientist Richard Owen.

1827 French mathematician Jean Baptiste Fourier introduces the greenhouse effect. He says Earth has the "effect of glass" in trapping heat from the Sun.

1830 Scotsman Sir Charles Lyell publishes his first edition of *Principles of Geology*. He suggests that the Earth is hundreds of millions of years old.

1831 English explorer James Clark Ross finds the magnetic north pole.

1837 US geologist James Dana suggests that landscapes are shaped by continuing forces of weathering and erosion, rather than by sudden catastrophic events such as earthquakes and volcanoes.

1840 Swiss-born scientist Louis Agassiz puts forward his theory of ice ages, and proposes that northern Europe was once covered in an ice sheet.

1872–76 HMS *Challenger*, under the direction of the British Admiralty and the Royal Society, makes the first thorough scientific exploration of the sea-bed. It travels 68,890 miles (127,600 km) on a four-year voyage mapping the world's oceans.

1874–75 Charles Sigsbee of the US Navy pioneers new methods of ocean-floor mapping (bathymetry) with his survey of the Gulf of Mexico on board the steamer *Blake*.

1880 English geologist John Milne invents the modern seismograph (instrument for measuring earthquakes).

1895 Swedish chemist Svante Arrhenius suggests that carbon dioxide added to the Earth's atmosphere helps to trap heat from the Sun, leading to global warming.

1903 Norwegian explorer Roald Amundsen makes the first voyage through the Northwest Passage (a sea corridor through the Arctic ice that connects the Atlantic and Pacific oceans..

1903 Norwegian scientist Kristian Birkeland explains how the northern lights are created.

1904 New Zealand scientist Ernest Rutherford explains radioactive decay. This discovery will lead to radiometric dating, a method used to calculate the age of rocks.

1906 Irish-born geologist Richard Oldham finds evidence for the Earth's iron core after studying seismic waves produced by earthquakes.

1909 Austrian geologist Eduard Suess writes *The Face of the Earth*, which explains how the Earth's processes shape the mountains and oceans. It also makes first mention of the ancient supercontinent Gondwanaland.

1910 Croatian scientist Andrija Mohorovicic studies seismic waves and discovers the boundary between the Earth's crust and mantle. This is known as the Mohorovicic discontinuity, or simply the Moho.

1911–12 Roald Amundsen leads the first successful expedition to reach the South Pole.

1912 German meteorologist Alfred Wegener publishes his continental drift theory, claiming that all the continents were once joined together in a supercontinent he called Pangaea. However, most scientists ignore it until the 1960s.

1920 Serbian scientist Milutin Milankovitch discovers the link between climate and solar radiation. He bases it on variations in Earth's orbit around the Sun—the "Milankovitch wobble."

1921 Norwegian meteorologist Vilhelm Bjerknes publishes the major study on the atmosphere. Bjerknes, who identifies air masses and fronts, is the father of modern weather forecasting.

1922 British physicist Lewis Richardson uses mathematical calculations to forecast the weather—a method that becomes practical much later, when computers are invented.

1924 US astronomer Edwin Hubble shows that nebulae (clouds where stars are formed) exist far beyond the Milky Way. In 1929 he shows that the Universe is expanding.

1927 Belgian astronomer Georges Lemaître proposes Big Bang theory of the origins of the Universe.

1931 English geologist Arthur Holmes publishes his geologic timescale. Based on radioactivity, he estimated the Earth to be 4 billion years old. Importantly, he proposed a theory of continental drift to explain Wegener's theory, suggesting convection currents in the mantle.were responsible for moving the tectonic plates.

1934 US naturalist Charles Beebe and engineer Otis Barton make a world record descent of 3,028 ft (923 m) in the bathysphere, pioneering deep-sea exploration.

1935 US physicist Charles Richter invents the Richter Scale for reporting the strength of earthquakes.

1935 US geophysicist Maurice Ewing takes the first seismic readings in the open sea. He links earthquakes to seafloor spreading from midocean ridges.

1936 Danish seismologist Inge Lehmann claims that the Earth's core has a solid inner and a liquid outer part. (Nuclear tests later prove her correct.)

1948–77 US mapmakers Marie Tharp and Bruce Heezen begin using sonar readings to map the ridges and other features of ocean floors. They publish the World Ocean Floor map in 1977. Their discoveries help scientists accept the tectonic plates theory in the 1960s.

1953 US scientist Clair Patterson calculates the age of the Earth. At 4.5 billion years, it is the first close estimate in the history of geology.

1959 US scientists on board the Coast and Geodetic Survey Ship *Pioneer* discover the Mid-Atlantic Ridge Rift Valley. This is the most significant bathymetric discovery made up to that time.

1959–62 US geologist Harry Hess's theory of seafloor spreading contributes to the acceptance of plate tectonics theory. He uses echo sounding to collect ocean floor profiles.

1963 British scientists Frederick Vine and Drummond Matthews realize that magnetic stripes in the crust along the midocean ridges show that the Earth's north-south magnetic polarity reverses regularly. Supports Hess's model of seafloor spreading.

1963 Canadian geologist John Tuzo Wilson introduces the theory of hot spots: rising plumes of magma in the Earth's mantle that heat the crust. He uses it to explain how islands such as the Hawaiian chain are created.

1964 *Alvin* makes its maiden voyage of exploration. This submersible, run by the Woods Hole Oceanographic Institution in the US, pioneers research and exploration in deep oceans. It provides the first observation of deep-sea hydrothermal activity.

1965 John Tuzo Wilson proposes a third type of plate boundary that connects the oceanic ridges and trenches: the transform-fault boundary. The best-known example of this is the San Andreas Fault zone.

1969 On July 20, the lunar module from the NASA Apollo 11 space mission puts the first man on the Moon.

1979 English scientist James Lovelock suggests that the Earth's systems work together as a giant, living organism. This idea is called the Gaia hypothesis.

1980 US scientists Luis and Walter Alvarez claim that a meteorite that struck near Mexico 65 million years ago could have created the climate change that killed off the dinosaurs.

1985 Scientists of the British Antarctic Survey record a springtime hole in the Earth's ozone layer over Antarctica.

1996 Scientists claim that a meteorite found in Antarctica has come from Mars. It contains structures which may prove that water—and life—once existed on the distant planet.

2004 NASA lands two robot vehicles, *Spirit* and *Opportunity*, on Mars to explore the planet's geology and to search for evidence of water and life.

GLOSSARY

Abyssal Relating to the deep ocean floor beyond the continental margin.

Air mass A large body of air with a uniform temperature.

Anticyclone A weather system in which winds circulate around a high pressure area.

Archipelago A group of islands forming a cluster or chain.

Asteroid A body of rock, smaller than a planet, that orbits the Sun. Most asteroids in the solar system are found in the asteroid belt, between the orbits of Jupiter and Mars.

Asthenosphere The weak layer of mantle immediately below the rigid lithosphere.

Atoll See *Coral reef.*

Atmosphere A layer of gas held around a planet or moon by its gravity.

Aurora The flickering lights produced over polar regions when solar wind particles hit the upper atmosphere. These lights are known as aurora borealis in the north, and aurora australis in the south.

Basalt Earth's most common volcanic rock, making up most of the crust under the oceans.

Biome The broadest classification of a community of plants and animals.

Biosphere All living organisms of the Earth and its atmosphere.

Black smoker see *Hydrothermal system.*

Caldera A collapsed crater at the summit of a volcano.

Comet A body of dust and ice that orbits the Sun.

Carbon The chemical element found in all living things, and many rocks and minerals. The carbon cycle is the transfer of carbon to and from the atmosphere.

Cirque A steep-sided, rounded hollow carved out at the head of a glacier.

Comet A body of dust and ice that orbits the Sun.

Condensation The transformation of a substance from a gas to a liquid.

Coniferous Cone-bearing evergreen trees, such as pines and firs, which usually have needlelike leaves. Coniferous trees make up the belt of forest around the lands of the far north, known as the boreal (or taiga in Eurasia).

Continent A very large landmass, for example Eurasia, Antarctica, or North America.

Continental margin The part of a continent along a coast and including the continental shelf and continental slope.

Continental shelf A shallow marine zone between dry land and the deep sea.

Continental slope A steep gradient between the continental margin and the deep sea-bed.

Convection The movement and circulation of gases and liquids in response to temperature changes.

Coral A plantlike animal made up of many small individuals—polyps—living together and sharing resources, such as food.

Coral reef A structure built up in shallow tropical seas by the activity of corals and other organisms. A reef that has grown on top of a sunken extinct volcano is called an atoll.

Core The intensely hot innermost layer of Earth, made up of a solid inner core and liquid outer core, both made of nickel and iron.

Crater The bowl-shaped opening at the summit of a volcano, through which an erupting volcano discharges gases and lava. Also a circular depression in a landscape caused by a meteorite impact.

Crust The outermost layer of solid Earth, consisting of continental and oceanic crust.

Crystal A solid, such as a mineral in a rock, whose atoms are arranged in an orderly pattern.

Current A flow of water or air.

Cyclone An area of low atmospheric pressure in which warm winds rise in a spiral. A tropical cyclone is another name for a hurricane.

Deciduous Relating to a tree that sheds its leaves in the fall.

Deep-sea trench A canyonlike depression in the ocean floor where one tectonic plate has slid beneath another.

Delta An area of sediment deposition built up by some rivers where they enter a sea or lake.

Deposition The laying down of material such as sand and gravel in new locations, usually by wind, water, or ice.

Desert A region where water is lost more rapidly than it is gained through precipitation.

Dune A mound of loose sand shaped by the wind.

Earthquake A sudden motion or trembling in the Earth caused by release along a fault.

Ecosystem A community of life-forms and their local environment.

El Niño A combined ocean and atmospheric event, taking place every 2–7 years, in which warm water currents in the Pacific Ocean flow east instead of west.

Equator An imaginary line around the middle of Earth that is at equal distance from the poles.

Erosion The general process that loosens, dissolves, or wears away the materials of Earth's crust and moves them from one place to another.

Eruption An outpouring of magma from within Earth. Magma that flows on Earth's surface is known as lava.

Fault A fracture in rock along which rock masses move – the source of earthquakes.

Fog Condensed droplets of water forming in the air at ground level.

Fossil The remains, imprint, or trace of a life-form preserved in rock.

Front The forward-moving edge of an air mass. An occluded front is a boundary in the atmosphere where cold air catches up with warm air and raises it off the ground.

Geothermal energy Electric power that is generated from steam produced by hot rocks, usually associated with volcanic activity.

Glaciation The formation and movement of glaciers or ice sheets.

Glacier A mass of of ice on land that flows slowly under gravity's influence. Valley glaciers flow down existing valleys. Piedmont glaciers form where several valley glaciers join at the base of a mountain range. An ice sheet is a vast layer of ice, that can cover large areas. Ice caps are smaller domes of ice covering a mountain.

Global warming The rise in temperature of Earth's atmosphere.

Greenhouse effect Trapping of the Sun's heat in the atmosphere by gases and particles.

Groundwater Precipitation that soaks into and is stored in the ground, rather than running off into rivers or evaporating.

Gyre A circular water current in an ocean.

Habitat The natural and usual living space of a plant or animal.

Hot spot A site of volcanic activity in Earth's crust created by rising magma from the mantle.

Humus Nutrient-rich matter, found in the upper layers of soil, that is produced from dead or decaying plants and animals.

Hurricane A destructive storm whipped up by energy released from rising warm winds.

Hydrothermal system Hot ground water that circulates in the Earth's crust. Igneous rocks are the main source of heat. When the heated water, enriched with dissolved minerals, escapes from the seafloor it produces discolored springs, known as "black smokers." The land equivalent is known as a hot spring.

Ice age A cold period in Earth's history.

Iceberg A floating block of ice that has broken off a coastal glacier or ice sheet.

Icecap see *Glacier.*

Ice sheet see *Glacier.*

Igneous rock Rock formed when lava or magma cools and crystallizes.

Island arc A chain of volcanic islands created over sites of volcanic activity.

Isobar A contour line on a weather map that shows variations in atmospheric pressure.

Jet stream Fast, cold wind-current blowing at high altitude.

Lagoon A calm body of water enclosed by sandbanks or the reefs of a coral atoll.

Lahar A fast-flowing stream of loose ash, rock, and mud that runs off a volcano's side, commonly set off by heavy rainfall.

Landslide see *Mass movement.*

Lava Magma that erupts and flows on Earth's surface. It cools after eruption to form rock.

Lightning Discharge of electricity within a thundercloud or from a thundercloud to the ground. A stroke of lightning can heat the air to temperatures of up to 54,000°F (30,000°C).

Lithosphere The rigid, outermost part of the Earth's layers – includes the crust and uppermost part of the mantle.

Magma Molten rock below the Earth's surface.

Magnetosphere The magnetic forcefield around the Earth, created by movement of iron in the planet's core. It protects the Earth from the charged particles that stream out from the Sun.

Mantle The middle layer of Earth's three main layers, up to 1,800 miles (2,870km) thick.

Mass movement A movement of rock or soil to lower ground as a result of gravity. Includes landslides.

Mesosphere The layer of the atmosphere above the stratosphere.

Metamorphic rock Rock changed from its original state by heat and pressure.

Meteor A bright streak of light formed when a lump of space rock heats up on entering the Earth's atmosphere. Any space rock that strikes the Earth is called a meteorite.

Midocean ridge An underwater volcanic mountain range that forms along a diverging tectonic plate boundary.

Mineral A naturally occurring, inorganic solid with a regular internal composition. Earth's rocks are made up of minerals.

Oasis A place in a desert where the presence of groundwater near the surface allows vegetation to grow.

Occluded front see *Front.*

Ore A natural material from which valuable minerals can be profitably extracted.

Ozone A form of oxygen. It can occur at ground level, but is found mostly in a layer in the stratosphere, where it filters some of the Sun's harmful ultraviolet light.

Photosynthesis The process in which organisms use sunlight to convert carbon dioxide and water into oxygen and sugars.

Planet A large, spherical mass in space that orbits a sun.

Plate boundary The location in the Earth's crust where tectonic plates are in contact. There are three kinds of plate boundaries: convergent (where plates move together); divergent (where they move apart), and transform (where one is sliding past the other).

Precipitation Water that falls to the ground in the form of rain, hail, or snow.

Pressure system The variations in atmospheric pressure that affect the local weather. While high pressure usually produces clear, dry skies, low pressure can lead to rain, hail, or thunder.

Pyroclastic Relating to material such as ash (volcanic glass and rock) ejected by a volcanic eruption. A pyroclastic flow is a deadly avalanche of hot ash, rock, and gases.

Rain forest Forest with lush growth produced by high rainfall (above 98 in (2,500mm) a year).

Rift valley A depression in the Earth's crust formed when landmasses are moving apart.

Rock A hard substance made up of one or more minerals. Some volcanic rocks are glassy.

Sediment The particles of rock, mineral, or organic matter that are transported in streams before settling on marine, river, or lake beds.

Sedimentary rock Rock formed from sediment that has been buried and squeezed by pressure from above.

Seismic wave A shockwave produced by an earthquake.

Soil Loose surface material produced by the weathering of rock or sediment and the addition of humus.

Stalactite A cone-shaped structure created when groundwater deposits minerals on a cave roof. A stalagmite is a pedestal-shaped structure created when water drips from the tip of a stalactite and deposits minerals on a cave floor.

Star A massive ball of burning gases in space that produces heat and light from the nuclear reaction in its core. The Sun is our local star.

Stratosphere The layer of Earth's atmosphere above the troposphere.

Subduction The sinking of an oceanic plate beneath a neighboring plate at a tectonic plate boundary.

Tectonic plate Any one of about 17 pieces of the Earth's rigid shell (made up of the crust and uppermost part of the upper mantle) that drifts slowly over the planet's surface in a process known as plate tectonics.

Temperate A region at high latitudes affected by seasonal change.

Thermosphere The outermost layer of the Earth's atmosphere.

Tide The regular rise and fall of seawater on a coast, mostly governed by the pull of the Moon's gravity on the oceans.

Tornado A destructive whirling wind that forms between a cloud and the ground surface.

Troposphere The layer of the atmosphere that is closest to the Earth's surface.

Tsunami An ocean wave triggered by an earthquake, submarine landslide, or volcano.

Typhoon see *Hurricane.*

Volcano The site of an eruption of molten rock from within the Earth. The buildup of erupted lava usually produces a cone. A stratovolcano explosively ejects both lava and pyroclastic material and has steep sides. A shield volcano is produced when highly fluid lava flows spread out to form a broad, gently sloping mountain.

Wave A form of energy transfer through water, air, or earth.

Wavelength The distance between the crest (highest point) and trough (lowest point) of a wave.

Weathering The process by which rock is disintegrated and decomposed by wind, water, frost, and organisms on the Earth's surface.

INDEX

A page number in **bold** refers to the main entry for that subject.

A

aa lava 25
ablation 47
abyssal plain 75
acid pollution 41
accumulation 47
air 76
air currents 76
air masses **80**, 86
air pressure 77, 80
　map 84
Alaska
　1964 earthquake 28, **29**
　Chugach mountains 35
　glaciers 46, 47
albatross 69
Aleutian island arc 45
algae **16**, 45, 66, 75
alligators 63
Alps 81
Alvin 74
Amazon rain forest 56
Amazon River **50**
Andes 21, 35
Andromeda galaxy 8
animals 11, 15, 44, 54, 56, 57, 60, 68
Antarctica 10, 15, 47, **64–65**, 77
Appalachians 35
Aral Sea, Uzbekistan 63
archipelago 44
Arctic 47, **64–65**, 78
Arctic Circle 10, **64**
Arctic Ocean 15, **64**, 68
argon 76
　dating 16
asteroid belt 9
asteroids 9
asthenosphere 20, **23**
Atacama Desert 55, 83
Atlantic Ocean 68
atmosphere 9, 10, 14, **76–77**, 79, 82
atmospheric conditions 81
atmospheric pressure 73, 85
atolls 45
aurora australis 12
aurora borealis 12

B

bacteria 75
basalt 18, **19**, 38, 45
　lava **25**, 75
　ocean floor 19, 20
　volcanoes 23
batholiths 39
bats 52
Beaufort Scale **88–89**
bedrock 48
Big Bang 8
biomes 15
biosphere **14–15**
biotite 40
bison 61
black smokers 75
blue ice 47
boto 56
boulders 43
　erratic 47
breakers 70
broadleaf trees 58, 59
bromeliads 57
brown bear 58

C

cacti 55
calcite 41, 43, **52**, **53**
caldera 23, 24
California
　earthquake zone 31, 33
　earthquakes 28, 29, **33**
　flooding 72
　forest fires 81
camels 54, 78
canopy 56, **57**
carbon **14**, 15, 41
carbon cycle 14
carbon dioxide 14, 16, 43, 78
cargo vessels 69
cave paintings 52
caves **52–53**
CFCs 10
cheetah 60
cirques 46
cirrus clouds 82
clay 48
climate 15, 35, 44
　change **78–79**
clouds 69, 77, 80, **82**
coastal damage 73
　see also erosion
cold, extreme 78
comets 9
compass 12, **13**
cone-bearing trees 58
cones 58
coniferous trees 58
continental crust 18, 19
continental margins 44, 66, **67**, 75
continental plates 19, 20, 34
continental shelf 67, 75
continental slope 75
continents, movement of **21**
copepods 67
copper 40
coral atolls 45
coral reef 14, **45**, 66
corals 45, 75
core 12, **18**
Coriolis effect 89
crocuses 59
crops/croplands 48, 49, 61
crust **18**, 19, 20, 23, 34, **38**
crustaceans 66, 67
crystals **40–41**
cumulonimbus clouds 80, **82**, 83
cumulus clouds 82
currents **68**, 69, 72
cyclones 86, 88, 89

D

Darwin, Charles 45
day 10
debris flow 36
deep water 74
deltas 51
deposition **39**, 42, 62
depression 84
depth record, manned 74
deserts 15, **54–55**, 78, 81
　cold 54, 64
　hot 54
　plantlife 55
　rain-shadow 54, 55
　reclamation 55
　soil 49
　west coast 54, 55
diamond 41
dinosaurs 17
doldrums 80
dolerite 25

dolphin, freshwater 56
Doppler 87
Douglas fir **58**, 59
downcutting 43
dragonfly 62
drip tips 56
droughts 72
drusy quartz 41
dunes 55
Durdle Door, Dorset 43
Dustbowl 61
Duzce, Turkey **28**, 31

E

Earth 9
　age of **16–17**
　axis 10
　inside **18–19**
　orbit around Sun **10–11**
　rigid shell 18, 20
　rotation 10, 11
earthquakes 18, 21, **28–29**, **30–31**, 32
　and tsunamis 70, 71
　laser monitoring 33
　predicting 30
　seafloor 71
earthworms 48
echinoderms 66
El Niño **72–73**
elements 40
emergents 57
energy sources 69
ENSO 72–73
ephemeral rivers 51
epiphytes 57
equinox
　autumnal 11
　vernal (spring) 11
erosion 35, 37, 39, **42–43**
　chemical 43
　coastal 37, **43**, 52, 73
　riverbanks 37, 50, 62
　soil 48
erratics 47
Everglades, Florida 63
evergreen trees 56, 58
exfoliation 42
extinctions 17
eye of the storm 88, 89

F

farming/farmland 48, 51, 61, 63
fault lines/faulting 28, 32, 34
faults **28**, 29, 31, 32
　normal 28
　reverse/thrust 29
　strike-slip 28, 32
feldspar 40
ferns 17, 59
fertile 26, 51
fertilizers 48, 51, 61
fetch 70
fires 59, 61, 81
firn 47
fish 66, 68, 73
fishing/fishermen 69, 72
fissure vents 23
floodplains 51, 62
floods 50, **51**, 62, **72**
fog 81
folding **34**
fool's gold 41
forest fires 59, 81
forest floor **57**
forest soil 48, **49**

forests **15**
　boreal 58
　coniferous **58**
　deciduous 58, 59
　dry 56
　flooded 57
　monsoon 56
　wet 56
　see also temperate, tropical
fossils **16**, **17**, 21, 35, 38, 54, 79
fronts **80**
　cold 80
　occluded 80
　warm 80
frost 42, 43
frost wedging **38**, 39
fruits 57
Fujita Scale 87
fungi 48, 57

G

Gaboon viper 57
Galapagos Islands **45**, 75
galaxies 8, 9
galena 41
Ganges River delta 51
gases 24, 76
geologic time scale 16, 17
geothermal energy 25
geysers 25
glaciations 79
glaciers 43, **46–47**, 64
Glossopteris 21
gold 40
granite 35, 38, 39, **40**, 42
grasslands **15**, 48, **60–61**
gravity 9, 10, 11, 14
Great Ocean Conveyor 68
Great Plains 61
Great Storm, England 89
Greenland 47, 64
groundwater 52, 53
Gulf Stream, Florida 69
gyres 68, 69

H

hail/hailstones 83
Hawaii 70, 71
　volcanoes 22, **23**, 24
heat, extreme 78
herons 62
hibernation 58
high pressure 80, 81
Hilo, Hawaii 71
Himalayas 20, **34**, 35, 83
Homo sapiens 17
hoodoos 42, **43**
Horsehead nebula 9
hot spots **19**, 23, 45
hot springs 25, 68, 75
humans 17, 44, 65
humpback whale 65
humus 48, 49
Hurricane Andrew 88, 89
Hurricane Floyd 89
Hurricane Gilbert 89
hurricanes 77, 84, **88–89**
hydrothermal vents 75

I

ice **46**, 79, 82
　polar 14, 64
Ice Age 44, 79

ice caps **47**, 79
ice cores 64, 79
ice crystals 82, **83**
ice sheets **46–47**
icebergs 46, **47**, 64
igloos 65
igneous rock 23, **38**, **39**
Indian Ocean 68
Indonesia 44
　droughts 72
　volcanoes **22**, 27, 79
insects 57, 60
inshore waters 66
Inuit 65, **78**
iron 12, **13**, 18, **19**
island arc 45, 75
islands **44–45**
isobars 84

J

Johnson Sea Link 74
Jupiter 9, 12

K

karst landscape **43**, 53
katydid 57
Kilauea volcano, Hawaii **24**
Kobe earthquake 28, **30**
Köppen's system 78
krill 65

L

lahars 27
landmasses 21
landslides 23, **36–37**, 70, 71
lava 22, 23, **24–25**
　fluid 24, 25
　ropey 25
　runny 23, 25
lava lake 24
lava tubes 25
lead 41
leaf litter 57
leaves 56, 58
life-forms 14
light-years 8
lightning 83
limestone 41, **43**, 52
　caves **53**
lithosphere **18**, 20, 21
lobster 66
loggerhead turtle 13
low pressure 80, 84, 86, 88

M

magma 19, 20, 21, **22**, 24, 25, 35, 38
　chamber 23
magnetic fields 12, 13, 19
magnetic north 13
magnetic north and south poles 12, 13
magnetism **12–13**
magnetite 13
magnetosphere 12
magnets 12, 13
malaria 63, 73
mammals 17, 60
mammoth 17, 44
manatee 63
mantle **18**, 19

lower 18, 19
upper 18, 19, 20, 22
mare's tails 82
margins 44, 66, 67
Mariana Trench 74
marine iguana 45
marine life 66–67
Mars 9, 12
Mauna Loa, Hawaii 22, 23
Mercury 9
mesocyclone 86, 87
Mesosaurus 21
mesosphere 77
metamorphic rock 38, 39
meteorites 9, 17
meteorology 84
meteors 9, 77
craters 9, 17
midnight Sun 10
midocean ridges 20, 21, 75
migration 13
Milky Way 8
minerals 19, 40–41, 75
Mistral 81
Mojave Desert 81
molten rock 18
Moment Magnitude Scale 27
monsoon 35, 80, 82, 83
Moon 9, 10–11, 77
phases 11
moons 9
moraines 46
mosquitoes 63, 73
Mount Etna, Italy 24
Mount Everest, Himalayas 34
Mount Huascarán, Peru 37
Mount Pinatubo, Philippines 22, 27
Mount St. Elias, Alaska 35
Mount St. Helens 22, 23, 27, 79
Mount Vesuvius, Italy 22, 26, 30
mountains
highest 34
mountain building 34–35
mountain ranges 19, 34
and weather 35, 81
mud flows 27
mudslide 37
mysid shrimp 67

N

navigation 13
neap tides 11
nebulas 9
Neptune 9
New Zealand 44
nickel 18, 19
night 10
Nile River 50, 51
nitrogen 14, 58, 76
North Pole 10, 12
northern lights 12

O

oases 53, 55
ocean crust 18, 19
ocean floor 19, 20, 75
map 74
see also seafloor
ocean tides see tides
ocean zones 66
bathypelagic/deep ocean 66
deep-sea 66
mesopelagic 66
sunlit/photic 66, 67, 68
twilight 68
oceanic plates 19, 21, 22

oceans 14, 68–69
depths 74–75
major 68
temperature 73
see also currents, tides
Okushiri, Japan 71
olivine 19
open seas 66, 67
orbits 10, 11
ore 40
Organ Pipes, Namibia 25
organic matter 14, 15, 48, 59
oxygen 14, 15, 76, 77
ozone 10, 76, 77
hole 10, 77

PQ

Pacific Ocean 68, 70, 72, 73, 84
pagoda, Japanese 33
pahoehoe lava 25
palm trees 55
Palmieri, Luigi 30
Pammukale, Turkey 41
Pangaea 21
parrotfish 66
peatland 63
penguin, emperor 65
perennial river 51
peridotite 19
photosynthesis 14, 59
phytoplankton 67
piedmont lobe 47
pillow lava 25
pines 58
pitcher plants 57
Piton de la Fournaise, Réunion 23
planets 8, 9
plankton 65, 67, 68, 73
plants 14, 15, 45, 55, 56, 57, 64
plate boundaries 20, 21, 22, 28, 32
convergent 20, 21
divergent 20, 21
transform 20, 21
plates 18, 19, 20–21, 35, 74
Pluto 9
polar bears 64
polar regions 15, 46, 47
pollution 77
polyps 66
Pompeii 26
prairie dogs 61
prairies 61, 86
fires 61
precipitation 82–83
pumice 26
P-waves 30
pyrite 41
pyroclastic materials 22, 23, 26

R

radar 87
radiometric dating 16
radiosondes 85
rain cloud formation 82
rain/rainfall 14, 16, 50, 56, 60, 72, 80, 82
lowest/highest 83
rain forests 56–57
temperate 59
rainwater, and erosion 39, 42, 43
ranges, mountain 34
Red Sea 21
redwoods 59
remotely operated vehicles (ROVs) 74
Richter Scale 28–29
rift valley 19

Ring of Fire 71
rivers 43, 50–51, 62
longest 50
rock cycle 38
rockfalls 36
rocks 38–39, 42
and age of Earth 16–17
mantle 18, 19
rockslides 35
rope tornado 80
runoff 50

S

sable antelope 60
Saffir-Simpson Hurricane Scale 88
Sahara 15, 54
salars 55
salt/salts 14, 55, 68
San Andreas Fault, 21, 32–33
San Francisco 21, 32, 33, 81
Transamerica Pyramid 33
Santa Ana winds 81
Saturn 9
savannas 15, 60
scatterometer 84
scorpion 54
sea ice 64
sea, inland 53
sea salt 68
seafloor 22, 74, 75, 79
see also ocean floor
seamount 75
seashells 35
seasonal rivers 51
seasons 10, 11
seawater 68
seaweed 69
sedimentary rock 34, 35, 38, 39, 42, 43
sediments 39, 51
deep-sea core 79
seismic waves 30
seismograms 31
seismographs 27, 30, 31
Serengeti, Tanzania 60
Shanghai seaport 50
shield volcanoes 23, 24
Shinkai 6500 74
shipping 69
shockwaves 30, 70, 83
Sierra Nevada 35, 39
silt 51, 62
silver 40, 41
sinkholes 53
slumping 36
smog 77
snakes 17, 58
snow 47, 64, 83
snowflakes 83
soil 15, 26, 48–49, 61
erosion 49
horizons 48
profile 48
soil creep 36
solar energy 14
solar radiation 10, 76, 77
solar system 9, 76
solar wind 12
sonar 74
South Equatorial Current 73
South Pole 12, 64
Southern Ocean 64, 68, 69
Southern Oscillation 72, 73
space 8, 12, 76
sperm whale 68
spring tides 11
springs, underwater 53
squid 66
squirrel monkey 57

stalactites 41, 52, 53
stalagmites 53
starfish, gray 66
stars 8, 9
stormchasers 87
storms 69, 70, 72, 77
stratosphere 77
stratovolcanoes 19, 22–23
stratus clouds 82
stromatolites 16
Strombolian eruption 24
Sturt's desert pea 55
subduction 21, 75
zone 19
submersibles 74
robot 74, 75
subsoil 48
sulfuric acid 79
summer 10, 11
sunlight 10, 11
Sun 8, 10–11, 27, 64, 76, 78
supercell 86
Surtsey 45
swamps 62, 63
S-waves 30

T

tamarisk 55
Tambora, Indonesia 22, 27, 79
tectonic plates 20, 74
see also plates
temperate
forests 15, 58–59
grasslands 60–61
seasons 11
zone 80, 81, 86
temperature 27, 76, 77, 79, 80
ocean 73
termites 60
thermosphere 76, 77
Three Gorges Dam, Yangtze 51
thunder 83
thunderclouds 86, 87
thunderstorms 80, 82, 83, 88
tidal power stations 70
tides, ocean 10, 11
till 46
time periods 16
Titanic 74
topsoil 37, 48, 49
Tornado Alley 86
tornadoes 86–87
toucan, toco 57
trade winds 73, 80
travertine 41
treeline 64
trees 17, 58, 89
rain forest 56, 57
wetland 62
tremors 31, 32
trenches, seabed 19, 68, 75
Triangulum galaxy 8
Trieste 74
Tri-State Tornado 87
tropical
cyclones 88, 89
forest 15, 56–57
grasslands 60
soil 48
winds 73
troposphere 76, 77
Tsunami Warning System (TWS) 71
tsunamis 29, 70–71
risk area 71
Tuaregs 78
tundra 64
twisters 86
typhoons 84

U

ultraviolet (UV)
light 10
radiation 77
understory 57, 59
Universe 8–9
Uranus 9

V

valleys
hanging 43
U-shaped 39, 43, 46
V-shaped 43
Venus 9, 12
viperfish 67, 68
volatiles 24
volcanic
ash 24, 26, 27, 79
mountain range 21
rock 19, 22
Volcanic Explosivity Index 26–27
volcanoes 16, 18, 20, 22–23, 71
eruptions 24
famous 25
living with 26–27
timeline 26–27
undersea hot springs 68, 75
underwater 25

W

walruses 65
water 9, 14, 52, 76, 82
and erosion 42
ocean 68, 69
water cycle 14, 50, 69, 76
water table 53
water vapor 69, 76, 82, 87
waterlogging 37, 62
waterspout 87
wave
action 70
energy 70
power 70
waves 70–71
biggest 70
largest 71
weather 77, 78, 80–81
aircraft 85
balloons 85
buoys 73, 84, 85
forecasting 84–85
local 81
map 84
satellites 84
stations 64, 81, 85
weathering 42, 48
Wegener, Alfred 21
westerlies 80
wetlands 15, 62–63
whales 13, 65, 68
wheat 61
wind speed 88
winds 70, 73, 77, 80, 81, 86, 87
see also hurricanes
winter 10, 11
wolf, gray 58
woolly mammoth 17, 44
worms, deep-sea 75

XYZ

Yangtze River 50, 51
zooplankton 67

ACKNOWLEDGMENTS

Dorling Kindersley would like to thank Lynn Bresler for proofreading and the index; Margaret Parrish for Americanization; and Rosie O'Neill for editorial support.

Picture Credits

The publisher would like to thank the following for their kind permission to reproduce their photographs:

Abbreviations key:

t-top, b-bottom, r-right, l-left, c-center, a-above, f-far

0: Getty Images/Antony Edwards/James Balog; 1: NASA (c); 2: Alamy Images/Glen Allison (c); 3: Zefa Visual Media (c); 4: Alamy Images/Tom Pfeiffer; 6: NASA (cr); 7: NASA (cl); 8: Corbis/Bryan Allen (b), Science Photo Library/Detlev van Ravenswaay (tr), Science Photo Library/National Optical Astronomy Observatories (cr), Science Photo Library/National Optical Astronomy Observatories (cfr), Science Photo Library/Space Telescope Science Institute (c); 9: NASA (b), Science Photo Library/European Southern Observatory (tr), Science Photo Library/Francois Gohier (br); 10: Corbis/David Bartruff (b), DK Images/NASA (cfl), NASA (bl); 11: DK Images/NASA/Finley Holiday Films (b), Science Photo Library/John Heseltine (tr), Science Photo Library/John Heseltine (cra), Science Photo Library/John Heseltine (crb), Science Photo Library/John Heseltine (cfr), Science Photo Library/Victor Habbick Visions (ca); 12: Corbis/Kennan Ward (l), Image courtesy Earth Science World ImageBank/NASA/JPL (t), Image courtesy Earth Science World ImageBank/NOAA (br), Science Photo Library/Space Telescope Science Institute/NASA (tr); 13: Corbis/Brian A. Vikander (br), DK Images/Courtesy of The British Library (tr), DK Images/Stephen Oliver (l); 14: Corbis/George D Lepp (cr), Getty Images/Helena Vallis (bl); 15: Corbis/Bryan Allen (c), Corbis/Hubert Stadler (br), Science Photo Library/Alexis Rosenfeld (r), Science Photo Library/John Eastcott & Yva Momatiuk (cr), Getty Images/Nicolas Parfitt (crb); 16: Corbis/Jim Sugar (l), Corbis/Lester V Bergman (cl), Science Photo Library/Georgette Douwma (br); 17: Corbis/James L Amos (cl); Corbis/M L Sinibaldi (bl), Corbis/Peter Johnson (br), DK Images/Dave King/Courtesy of the National Museum of Wales (tr), DK Images/Harry Taylor /Natural History Museum (cr), Science Photo Library/D. van Ravenswaay (tl); 19: Corbis/Richard Cummins (car), GeoScience Features Picture Library/Dr. B. Booth (cal), Getty Images/Greg Pease (cla); 20: Corbis/Jason Burke/Eye Ubiquitous (tl); 21: Corbis (tl), Corbis (cl); Corbis/Original image courtesy of NASA (cfl), Corbis/Kevin Schafer (bl), DK Images/Harry Taylor/Courtesy of the Royal Museum of Scotland, Edinburgh (cb), DK Images/Harry Taylor/Courtesy of the University Museum of Zoology, Cambridge (br); 23: Corbis/Bouhet Richard (br), Corbis/Roger Ressmeyer (tr), US Geological Survey/USGS (cr); 24: Science Photo Library/Bernard Edmaier (tr); USGS (cl); 25: Corbis/Hans Strand (br); Corbis/Ralph White (cl), DK Images/Gables (tr), Science Photo Library/G. Brad Lewis (clb), US Geological Survey/J.B. Judd (tl), US Geological Survey/R. L. Christiansen (bl); 26: Corbis/Jonathan Blair (bl), Corbis/Yann Arthus-Bertrand (c), DK Images/James Stevenson/Courtesy of the Museo Archeologico Nazionale di Napoli (c); 27: Corbis/Yann Arthus-Bertrand (br), Powerstock/Phillippe Bourseiller (cr), Science Photo Library/Robert M. Carey, Science Photo Library/NOAA (tr), US Geological Survey/USGS (cl); 28: Corbis/Lloyd Cluff (cfr), Image courtesy Earth Science World ImageBank (bl), Image courtesy Earth Science World ImageBank/Chris Keane/American Geological Institute (br), Panos Pictures (cl); 29: Corbis (tl), Corbis/Bettmann (br), US Geological Survey (bl), US Geological Survey/C. E. Meyer (cl); 30: DK Images/John Lepine/Science Museum, London (bl), Panos Pictures/Jim Holmes (tr); 31: Corbis/Reuters (t), Science Photo Library/Carlos Munoz-Yague/Eurelios (cl), Science Photo Library/NASA (cr); 32: Corbis/Lloyd Cluff; 33: Corbis (t), Corbis/Bettmann (cl), Corbis/George Hall (c), Corbis/Roger Rossmeyer (br); 34: Alamy Images/Colin Monteath/Worldwid Picture Library (c); 35: Alamy Images/Chris Howes/Wild Places Photography (cfr), Corbis/Pablo Corral Vega (br), DK Images/Colin Keates/Courtesy of the Natural History Museum, London (tr), Image courtesy Earth Science World ImageBank/Bruce Molnia, Terra Photographics (clb), Image courtesy Earth Science World ImageBank/Martin Miller/University of Oregon (tl), Image courtesy Earth Science World ImageBank/National Park Service (cb); 36: Corbis/Lloyd Cluff (c), Science Photo Library/Gary Hincks (bl), US Geological Survey/R. L. Schuster (c); 37: Corbis/Kike Arnal (cr), Lowell Georgia (br), US Geological Survey/Tom Lynch (tc), US Geological Survey/Tom Lynch (tr); 38: DK Images/Andreas Einsiedel (br), DK Images/Colin Keates (br), DK Images/Colin Keates (br), Image courtesy Earth Science World ImageBank (bl), Image courtesy Earth Science World ImageBank/Martin Miller/University of Oregon (cl), Tony Waltham Geophotos (cl), Tony Waltham Geophotos (l); 39: Tony Waltham Geophotos (c); 40: Image courtesy Earth Science World ImageBank/ASARCO (cbl), Science Photo Library/Dirk Wiersma (r); 41: Image courtesy Earth Science World ImageBank/Dr. Richard Busch (tr), Image courtesy Earth Science World ImageBank/Stonetrust Inc (bc), GeoScience Features Picture Library/Dr. B. Booth (c), Science Photo Library/Simon Fraser (br); 42: Corbis/Joseph Sohm/ChromoSohm Inc. (t), Corbis/William Manning (bc); 43: Corbis/Brian A. Vikander (tr), Corbis/John M. Roberts (cr), Corbis/Tiziana & Gianni Baldizzone (br); 44: Corbis/Nik Wheeler (b), Getty Images/Stone/Paul Chesley (bl), Science Photo Library/M-Sat Ltd. (car), Science Photo Library/Worldsat International (cfl), Still Pictures/Qinetiq (tcr); 45: Corbis/Galen Rowell (tl), GeoScience Features Picture Library/Dr. B. Booth (c), Still Pictures/Gunter Ziesler (r), Still Pictures/Steve Kaufman (cl), Still Pictures/Truchet/UNEP (bc); 46: Bryan And Cherry Alexander Photography/J Hyde (l); 47: Bryan And Cherry Alexander Photography (tr), Corbis (tl), Corbis/Chris Rainier (bl), Corbis Ralph/A. Clevenger (br), Science Photo Library/British Antarctic Survey (bc), Science Photo Library/Tony Craddock (cl); 48: Corbis/Richard Hamilton Smith (r); 49: Corbis/Julia Waterlow/Eye Ubiquitious (tr); DK Images/Alan Watson (cl), Image courtesy Earth Science World ImageBank/NASA Visible Earth (br), National Resources Conservation (tc), National Resources Conservation (c), National Resources Conservation (cb), Science Photo Library/David Nanuk (bl); 50: Corbis/Dean Conger (t), Corbis/Layne Kennedy (br), Corbis/Nik Wheeler (bc), Corbis/Wolfgang Kaehler (bl); 51: Corbis (tl), Corbis/Christine Osborne (cl), Corbis/Richard Hamilton Smith (cl), Corbis/Roger Wood (tr), Corbis/Roger Wood (cl), Panos Pictures (cr), Panos Pictures (br); 52: Corbis/David Muench (r), Corbis/Robert Gill/Papilo (c), Zefa Visual Media/G Rossenbach (bl), 53: Corbis/Reuters (br), Zefa Visual Media/G. Rossenbach (bl); 54: Corbis/Michelle Westmorland (l); 55: Nature Picture Library/Rhonda Klevansky (r), Corbis (t), Getty Images/Stone/Mark Wagner (c); 56: Corbis/Jeremy Horner (bl), Science Photo Library/Gregory Ochocki (br); 57: Corbis/Kevin Schafer (br), Corbis/Michael & Patricia Fogden (cr); 58: Still Pictures/P. Labarbe (l); 59: Corbis/John M. Roberts (tl), Woodfall Wild Images (bl), Woodfall Wild Images (r); 60: DK Images/Gables (cr), DK Images/Jerry Young (br), Getty Images/Nicholas Parfitt (c); 61: Corbis/Bettmann (br), Corbis/W. Wayne Lockwood, M.D. (t), DK Images/Peter Anderson (cfr); 62: Science Photo Library/Martin Dohrn (clb); 63: Alamy Images/Robert Harding World Imagery (clb), Oxford Scientific Films/Daniel Cox (crb), Still Pictures/F.Ardito/UNEP (tr), Getty Images/Randy Wells (crb); 64: Corbis/Graham Neden/Ecoscene (cbr); 64-65: Corbis/Hans Strand (tr), Getty Images/Peter Scoones (b); 65: DK Images/Neil Fletcher (crb); 66: Corbis/Robert Yin (cl), Corbis/Stephen Frink (clb); 66-67:Getty Images/Mike Kelly (c); 67: Science Photo Library/Andrew Syred (tcr), Science Photo Library/B. Murton/Southampton Oceanography Centre (cr), Science Photo Library/British Antarctic Survey (tc), Science Photo Library/Laguna Design (tr), Getty Images/Mike Kelly (tl), Getty Images/Peter David (cb); 68: Still Pictures/Peter Schickert (tr); 68-69: Corbis/Robert Y. Ono (b); 69: Corbis/Jim Sugar (tr), Corbis/Jonathan Blair (clb), Corbis/Natalie Fobes (cla); Corbis/Philip Gould (bl), Corbis/Tom Brakefield (cbr), Science Photo Library/NOAA (tl); 70: Science Photo Library/Martin Bond (cfl); 71: Associated Press (crb), Corbis/Lloyd Cluff (bl), NOAA (tc); 72: Corbis/Hubert Stadler (tr), Pa Photos/EPA (bc); 73: Corbis/Richard T. Nowitz (bc),Corbis/Vince Streano (br), Seapics.com/Mark Conlin (bl), NOAA (tl), Science Photo Library/R.B.Husar/NASA (tr); 74: Corbis/Chris McLaughlin (tr), Corbis/Layne Kennedy (clb), Science Photo Library/Colin Cuthbert (cfl), Science Photo Library/W.Haxby, Lamont-Doherty Earth Observatory (bc); 75: Nature Picture Library/Florian Graner (cb), Stephen Low Productions Inc (br); 76: European Space Agency (tr), Science Photo Library/Mike Boyatt /Agstock (clb), Zefa Visual Media (tl); 77: Alamy Images/ImageState (bl), Science Photo Library/NASA (c), Getty Images/Arnulf Husmo (cfr), Zefa Visual Media (cb); 78: Corbis/Jacques Langevin (tl), Powerstock/Peter Adama (bl), Science Photo Library/British Antarctic Survey (br); 78-79: Science Photo Library/NASA(tl); 79: Corbis/Gary Braasch (crb), Corbis/Lowell Georgia (tr); 80: Corbis (tl); 81: Corbis/Reuters (clb), Corbis/Richard Cummins (cfr), Corbis/Roger Ressmeyer (t), Getty Images/Angelo Cavalli (cfl); 82: Corbis/Reuters (l), DK Images/Brian Cosgrove (cr), DK Images/Brian Cosgrove (crb); 83: Corbis/Hubert Stadler (clb); Corbis/Rob Matheson (r), Corbis/Tiziana and Gianni Baldizzone (cbl), Science Photo Library/Jim Reed (c), Science Photo Library/Ted Kinsman (ca); 84: NASA (clb), Science Photo Library (br); Science Photo Library/NASA (tr); 85: Alamy Images/Michael Dwyer (bl), aviation-images.com/Mark Wagner (tr), Science Photo Library/British Antarctic Survey (cla), Science Photo Library/British Antarctic Survey (cfr), Science Photo Library/Hank Morgan (bc); 86: Oxford Scientific Films/Warren Faidley (c), Oxford Scientific Films/Warren Faidley (cr), Oxford Scientific Films/Warren Faidley (cfr); 87: Corbis (tl), Corbis/Jim Reed (cfr), Corbis/Ray Soto (cfl), Hulton Archive/Getty Images (cra); 88-89: Corbis/Reuters (b); 89: Science Photo Library/Chris Sattlberger (cb), Getty Images/Ed Pritchard (br); 94: Corbis/Bill Varie (l); 95: Corbis/Bill Varie (r).

Jacket images
Front: Corbis: Steve Wilkings (cfr); Science Photo Library: Krafft/Explorer (cr), NASA (cl). **Spine:** Corbis: Steve Wilkings. **Back:** Corbis: (cl); Science Photo Library: Mehau Kulyk (cr).

All other images © Dorling Kindersley. For further information see: **www.dkimages.com**